CW00521517

CONTE

Spelling and vocabulary

Introduction

The intention of this book is to provide information about the English spelling system and to explain something of the language structures which influence spelling. It would be impossible to learn the correct spelling of every word as a discrete entity, but it is possible, if you understand how words work, to generalise, to make analogies and to perceive patterns. The English language and the history of spelling is a fascinating study in its own right and it is clear that children who are interested in words are more likely to be able to spell effectively. At the same time, an interest in words promotes the development of increasingly wider vocabulary and the desire to use it.

Many children become so anxious about the correct spelling of the words they use that they begin to see this as the only important aspect of their writing. Their writing – what they want to express – is often restricted by unwillingness to risk making mistakes and so they use only vocabulary they know how to spell. Teachers need to understand that children's errors provide much information about a child's current thinking and understanding, which can be analysed and used in teaching. Especially in the early stages, errors should be seen as evidence of development which needs to be taken further. For teachers to do this they need the background knowledge themselves so that they can intervene and explain misconceptions. This approach to spelling was uncommon in the past so many teachers do not have this knowledge. This book will help to fill some of the gaps.

POCKET GUIDES

TO THE PRIMARY CURRICULUM

Spelling and vocabulary

Liz Laycock

Provides the knowledge you need
to teach the primary curriculum

Author
Liz Laycock

Editor
Dodi Beardshaw

Assistant Editor
Christine Harvey

Cover design
Joy Monkhouse
Rachel Warner

Designer
Erik Ivens

Illustrations
Garry Davies

Cover photograph
Calvin Hewitt

The publishers would like to thank **Barefoot Books Ltd** for the use of a text extract from *Princess Prunella and the Purple Peanut* by Margaret Atwood. Text © 1995, Margaret Atwood, Illustrations © 1995, Maryann Kovalski (1995, first published in Great Britain by Barefoot Books Ltd).
The Centre for Language in Primary Education for the use of a table from *Whole to Part Phonics* by Dombey, Moustafa et al. © 1998, CLPE (1998) CLPE, Weber Street, London SE1 8QW. info@clpe.co.uk.
Faber and Faber Ltd for the use of seven lines from 'Gulls' from *The Mermaid's Purse* by Ted Hughes © Ted Hughes (Faber and Faber Ltd).
Oxford University Press for the use of the definition of 'spell' from *The Concise Oxford Dictionary* (10th revised edition 2001) © 2001, Oxford University Press (2001, OUP).
The Random House Group for an extract from *Pass the Jam, Jim* by Kaye Umansky © Kaye Umansky (Bodley Head/Red Fox).
Thames and Hudson Ltd for the use of two lines of Jarman handwriting examples from p 27 of *Practical Guide to Children's Handwriting* by Rosemary Sassoon © 1983, Rosemary Sassoon (1983, Thames and Hudson).

Every effort has been made to trace copyright holders and the publishers apologise for any omissions.

Published by Scholastic Ltd,
Villiers House,
Clarendon Avenue,
Leamington Spa,
Warwickshire CV32 5PR
www.scholastic.co.uk

Printed by Cox & Wyman Ltd, Reading

Text © 2001 Liz Laycock
© 2001 Scholastic Ltd

1 2 3 4 5 6 7 8 9 0   2 3 4 5 6 7 8 9 0 1

British Library Cataloguing-in-Publication Data
A catalogue record for this book is available from the British Library.

ISBN 0-439-01990-7

Designed using Adobe Pagemaker

The ability to spell accurately is socially very important; it is seen as an indication of a child's success in literacy. It is important to remember, however, that being able to spell words accurately is not an indicator of intelligence or ability. Many people have difficulty with spelling sometimes, especially if they are using new, unfamiliar vocabulary. What is needed is not to tell learners that they must 'improve' their spelling, but to *teach* children about words and give them strategies to learn how to spell them. This is the intention underlying the requirements in the National Curriculum for English and exemplified in the National Literacy Strategy Framework for Teaching. There are many factors which must be considered in teaching children to spell. As well as knowing about letter–sound correspondences children must be helped to develop visual memory and strategies because good spellers draw on knowledge of visual patterns as well as understandings about the structure of the language. Children need to be helped to 'look with intent' (Peters, 1990) and to be able to do this teachers need to understand the underlying logic and patterns of English orthography. Informed teachers can draw on a wide range of approaches matched to the developmental needs of their pupils, rather than following exclusively a narrow, prescriptive path.

The English language is constantly evolving and changing. The beginnings of English lie deep in the past and it absorbed elements of many other languages as invaders settled in these islands. Vocabulary from distant lands has been incorporated and new vocabulary coined for creative, medical, technological and scientific concepts and developments. This process continues; spelling and usage changed in the past and they continue to do so now. Teaching children *about* the language – about its history, about the principles underlying the spelling system, about words and their meanings and about the ways in which writers use the language to communicate ideas and feelings – is vital if they are to become successful writers and spellers themselves. This field of study does not have to be tedious; the teacher's own knowledge and enthusiasm will play a big part in developing children's interest. When their interest has been kindled children will be keen to find out more.

The teaching ideas in this book reflect the requirements of the National Curriculum and the National Literacy Strategy materials. Activities are suggested which set out to encourage children to play with language and to develop interest and curiosity through an investigative approach. The best resource for language study, play and investigation is the language itself, though some resources are suggested at the end of each chapter.

A note about letters and sounds in this book
When letters are referred to, they are shown in italic: *c, ch, h, th, -igh, ea, ou, ay.*

When the sounds of these (phonemes) are referred to they are shown in italic between oblique strokes: */k/, /ch/, /h/, /th/, /ie/, /ee/, /ow/, /ae/.*

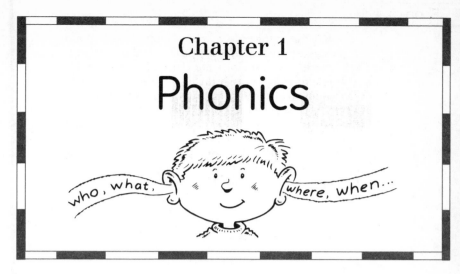

Chapter 1
Phonics

This chapter sets out to consider phonics and spelling. English is not a phonically regular language so the process of learning letter–sound correspondences and using this knowledge to decode words is not as straightforward as it may seem. The alphabet of 26 letters has to represent the 44 or so sounds of the language, so there are many ways in which letters must be combined in order to represent or spell these sounds. Consonants and vowels are combined in different ways to represent different sounds.

Teachers need to reflect upon the most effective ways of enabling learners to read and write. In recent years there has been a much greater emphasis on phonic instruction for young learners; the National Literacy Strategy Framework for Teaching in the Word Level work emphasises 'phonological awareness, phonics and spelling' as well as 'graphic knowledge and spelling'. Teachers need to understand how the English alphabetic system works and the terminology involved so that explanations will be clear and confusion avoided.

Phonics terminology

Subject facts

Phonics has been defined as 'the relationship between print symbol and sound patterns' (DfEE,1995). It would perhaps be more accurate to use the term *grapho-phonic* to describe this relationship because it is about both the written symbol (grapheme) and the sound (phoneme). The term *phonic*, however, is an abbreviated way of expressing this relationship. Teachers often speak of 'teaching phonics'; by this they mean they are teaching about letter–sound correspondences. In approaches to reading and spelling which are predominantly phonic, children are asked to 'sound out' words in reading and are asked 'what sounds can you hear?' to spell. Traditional phonics teaching over-simplifies the relationship between the sound in a word and the written symbol and takes no account of regional variation in accents, for example the varying pronunciation of *grass* and *look* in different parts of the British Isles!

A *phoneme* is the smallest unit of sound which changes the meaning of a word and *phonology* is the study of the sound systems of the language as they relate to meaning. For example, the word *pig* is made up of three phonemes: *p–i–g*. Each phoneme is represented by a single letter. If any one of these phonemes is changed, the meaning is changed.

> p–i–g = pig (a domesticated mammal used for food)
> b–i–g = big (of a large size)
> p–e–g = peg (a piece of wood used for holding together parts of a framework)
> p–i–n = pin (a thin piece of metal with a sharp point)

Each of these changes of one phoneme produces a new word with a completely different meaning.

Crystal (1995) says, 'When we talk about the sound system of English, we are referring to the number of phonemes that are used in a language and to how they are organised.' Although some simple words can be separated quite easily into individual phonemes, English spelling does not consistently work on the basis of one letter representing one phoneme (see below).

Each of the phoneme changes in the words above is represented by a different grapheme. A *grapheme* is the written representation of a sound (phoneme) and may consist of one or more letters (NLS, 1998). A grapheme can be a single letter or a combination of letters. For example, in the word *hat*, there are three graphemes: *h* + *a* + *t* , each representing a single phoneme.

In the word *that*, there are also three graphemes: *th* + *a* + *t*. The first grapheme, *th*, consists of two letters representing the phoneme /th/; the other two phonemes /a/ and /t/ are represented by one letter each.

Crystal (1995) defines a grapheme as 'the smallest contrastive unit in the writing system of a language' and he includes punctuation marks in this system because a punctuation mark can show difference (contrast) in meaning.

Phonemic awareness relates to the listener's awareness of the individual sounds in spoken language. The term is commonly used in describing a child's ability to distinguish the phonemes or separate sounds in a word. Recent research (for example, Bryant, 1993) into children's reading development has shown that phonemic awareness develops once children begin to read and write, rather than being a prerequisite.

Phonological awareness is an umbrella term for a general awareness of sounds. This would include the child's ability to hear rhymes as well as phonemic awareness.

This terminology is in constant use in both National Curriculum and National Literacy Strategy documentation. Teachers need to use terms accurately in order to describe what they are doing and to record children's progress. It is not necessary for young children to be taught this terminology, although the term *phoneme* is increasingly being used instead of the more general *sound* and children do seem to enjoy knowing this word.

Why you need to know these facts

Graphemes can appear in a variety of forms; each one of the forms is known as a *graph*. There are thousands of possibilities for the shape and form of a graph. Figure 1 shows some variations for the grapheme *b*.

Amazing facts

B,b B,b B,b **B,b** B,b B,b B,b B,b **B,b** B,b B,b B,b

Figure 1

The terms *phonic* and *phonetic* are often used interchangeably. However, they do actually mean different things.

Phonetics is the study of the way speech sounds are made, received and transmitted by humans. Phoneticians have devised sets of symbols, which are not letters of the alphabet, to identify speech sounds – these are called *phonetic symbols* (see Figure 2).

The most common usage of these can be found in dictionaries where they indicate how a word should be pronounced.

Common misconceptions

> **Phonetic dictionary entry**
>
> discontinue   (ˌdɪskən'tinjuː)
>
> write   (raɪt)
>
> The stress pattern is marked with the symbols ' for primary stress and ˌ for secondary stress. Words are transcribed in the International Phonetic Alphabet (IPA).
>
> **Figure 2**

The term is also used when describing a stage in a child's spelling development. A teacher may say that a child has spelled a word phonetically, meaning that the speller has identified the sounds he/she can hear in a word and has represented these with a logical grapheme. The grapheme used to represent the phoneme may not be the conventional one, so the word will not be spelled 'correctly', for example, *ced (seed), flowr (flower), bise (busy), ov (of), becos (because)*.

Teaching ideas

Activities which develop children's phonological awareness generally include games with rhymes and alliteration.

• Include the singing of a range of rhymes and songs as part of daily routines with young children. These should include traditional nursery rhymes, short rhythmic poems, counting rhymes, finger rhymes and songs or rhymes which include clapping, stamping and other types of body percussion.

• Once a rhyme or song is familiar to a group, leave gaps in your singing or reading and invite the children to fill in the missing rhyming word.

• Ask the children to tell you which pairs of words rhyme in familiar rhymes such as 'Humpty Dumpty', 'One, Two, Buckle My Shoe', 'Little Jack Horner'.

• Create a screened area and ask children to listen to everyday sounds made behind the screen, such as tearing paper, and pouring or splashing water, and to identify what they are. This can be extended by making tape-recordings of familiar sounds such as animal noises, different machines, people speaking and asking children to identify these.

• Have musical instruments available for children to explore the different sounds and use these in sessions with songs.

• Use the children's names and ask them to tell you which ones begin with the same sound; call out all the children whose name begins with a particular consonant phoneme such as /b/ or /s/.

• Ask children to identify the odd one out in groups of words beginning with the same sound or which rhyme. For example, 'sing, mouth, song, skip', 'bread, butter, cake, biscuit', emphasizing the initial phoneme so that it is drawn to the children's attention. Vary the position of the odd one out, for example, 'cat, mat, sat, dog', 'man, can, cup, fan'.

The sound system of the English language

Subject facts

The English writing system is alphabetic so the teaching of reading and spelling can seem a simple matter of matching letters to sounds. It is not simple, though, because we have 26 letters in our alphabet but over 44 different sounds (phonemes) have been identified. There is, however, a clear link between the *phonology* (the sound system of the language) and the *graphology* (the written symbols representing the sounds) and this is the starting point for young children.

The written alphabet
The shapes of the lower-case letters in the modern alphabet owe much to the scribes of the Roman Empire and their need to develop efficient handwriting. Figure 3 shows the runic alphabet in which some Old English was written.

Later Roman	Runic
A	ᚴ
B	ᛒ
D	ᛞ
E	ᛖ
L	ᚱ
M	ᛗ
P	ᚴ
T	↑

Figure 3

Christian missionaries and Roman scribes introduced the Roman alphabet very quickly once they arrived in Britain. The 23 Latin letters were attached systematically to the English sound system and additional symbols were created to represent unfamiliar sounds. These Anglo-Saxon symbols were later replaced by combinations of letters (for example, *th*) and the creation of a new letter, *w*. In the late Middle Ages, two new letters, *v* and *j* were introduced to distinguish them from *u* and *i* with which they had been interchangeable. The result of this is the 26-letter alphabet we now use.

Vowels and consonants

Of these 26 letters, 5 are called *vowels* and 21 are called *consonants*. As soon as writers begin to encode spoken language into writing, it becomes apparent that there are more sounds in English than can be encoded by these letters. Although there is a much closer match between the consonant letters and consonant sounds, the vowel sounds are much more complex. David Crystal (1995) has shown that:

> *there are in fact some 20 or so vowels in most accents of English (the exact number often depending on the way the system is analysed), and their sound qualities can vary from accent to accent.*

In spelling terms, matters are further complicated by the fact that, in English, these vowel phonemes are represented by differing letter combinations.

Crystal (1995) provides a table to 'show the set of vowels found in English'. He gives the phonetic transcriptions of these vowels. Figure 4 shows one of the transcription systems and his word list to demonstrate the variety in the spelling of the same sound.

sea, feet, me, field	iː
him, big, village, women	i
get, fetch, head, Thames	e
sat, hand, ban, plait	æ
sun, son, blood, does	ʌ
calm, are, father, car	a
dog, lock, swan, cough	ɔ
all, saw, cord, more	ɔː
put, wolf, good, look	u
soon, do, soup, shoe	uː
bird, her, turn, learn	ɜː
the, butter, sofa, about	ə
ape, waist, they, say	ei
time, cry, die, high	ai
boy, toy, noise, voice	ɔi
so, road, toe, know	ou
out, how, house, found	au
deer, here, fierce, near	iə
care, air, bare, bear	ɛə
poor, sure, tour, lure	uə

Figure 4

Note: this list is based on Received Pronunciation (RP). Some words may be pronounced differently in a different regional accent.

This set of symbols is the one devised by a British phonetician, Daniel Jones (1881–1967), for his pioneering description of English Received Pronunciation (RP). He was recognised, in the 1920s, as the British authority on phonetics. He was the linguist/phonetician who first defined the characteristics of RP – the accent of the highly educated. Phonetic symbols are used extensively in teaching English as a foreign language, in order to indicate the precise differences in the pronunciation of the vowel sounds of English. They are also used by linguists to transcribe the actual sounds of the language when it is spoken, because precise differences cannot be represented by the limited vowel letters of combinations of letters of the traditional alphabet.

The National Literacy Strategy training materials (1998 and 2000) identify the following vowel phonemes and their more usual graphemic representations. The sounds (phonemes) are distinguished from the letters by a slash on either side: / /.

/a/	cat
/e/	peg, bread
/i/	pig, wanted
/o/	log, want
/u/	plug, love
/ae/	pain, day, gate, station
/ee/	sweet, heat, thief, these
/ie/	tried, light, my, shine, mind
/oe/	road, blow, bone, cold
/ue/	moon, blue, grew, tune
/oo/	look, would, put
/ar/	cart, fast (regional)
/ur/	burn, first, term, heard, work
/or/	torn, door, warn (regional)
/au/	haul, law, call
/er/	wooden, circus, sister
/ow/	down, shout
/oi/	coin, boy
/air/	stairs, bear, hare
/ear/	fear, beer, here

The NLS uses a simplified representation of the phonemes, drawing on the common digraphs, to represent the sound, rather than standard phonetic transcriptions. This can sometimes be confusing to those familiar with recognised phonetic symbols.

The NLS symbols are also designed largely to represent the sounds produced in the RP accent. There is some attempt to acknowledge regional variation (in /ar/ and /or/) but variations are not noted (for example, *look* is indicated as having a pronunciation like *would* or *put* – /oo/; but in Lancashire *look* would be much closer to *moon* or *blue* – /ue/). It is vowel sounds that are most likely to vary from region to region.

The discrepancies are not so great in the representation of consonants. The NLS list of consonant phonemes and their more usual graphemic representations is set out as follows:

/b/	**b**aby
/d/	**d**og
/f/	**f**ield, **ph**oto
/g/	**g**ame
/h/	**h**at
/j/	**j**udge, **g**iant, bar**g**e
/k/	coo**k**, **qu**i**ck**, mi**x**, **Ch**ris
/l/	**l**amb
/m/	**m**onkey, co**mb**
/n/	**n**ut, **kn**ife, **gn**at
/p/	**p**aper
/r/	**r**abbit, **wr**ong
/s/	**s**un, mou**se**, **c**ity, **sci**en**ce**
/t/	**t**ap
/v/	**v**an
/w/	**w**as
/wh/	**wh**ere *(regional)*
/y/	**y**es
/z/	**z**ebra, plea**s**e, i**s**
/th/	**th**en, **th**in
/ch/	**ch**ip, wa**tch**
/sh/	**sh**ip, mi**ss**ion, **ch**ef
/zh/	trea**s**ure
/ng/	ri**ng**, si**n**k

Regional variations

There is recognition in this list for the regional variation which distinguishes */w/* from */wh/*.

However, there is not the same recognition that the digraph */ng/* is more likely to be two separate phonemes in words such as *ring, sing* and *singing* in accents in parts of Britain! (See pages 19–22 for further discussion on vowels and consonants.)

Digraphs and trigraphs

It will be apparent from these respective lists of vowel and consonant phonemes, that there have to be several combinations of letters in order to create graphemes to represent all the phonemes of the English language. These combinations, both vowel and consonant, are known as *digraphs* (two graphs or symbols) or *trigraphs* (three graphs or symbols).

The significant thing about digraphs and trigraphs is that they combine letters to represent a single sound (phoneme), unlike *consonant clusters* or *blends* which are separate phonemes blended together. Here are some examples:

> **sh–ee**–p   a consonant digrap*h* (*sh*), representing a single phoneme */sh/*; a vowel digraph (*ee*), representing the single phoneme */ee/* and a single grapheme (*p*), representing the phoneme */p/*.
>
> n–**igh**–t   a single grapheme (*n*) representing the phoneme */n/*; a mixed vowel + consonant trigraph (*igh*) representing the phoneme */ie/* and a single grapheme (*t*) representing the phoneme */t/*.
>
> **spl**–a–**sh**   a consonant blend at the beginning with three separate phonemes */s/, /p/, /l/*, a further single grapheme (*a*) representing the phoneme */a/* and a consonant digraph (*sh*) at the end representing the phoneme */sh/*.

The common consonant digraphs are usually introduced to children early on, alongside the single initial consonants. These are:

ch	sh	th (voiced)	th (unvoiced)	wh
chain	ship	they	three	what
chair	shirt	this	think	wheel
church	shut	there	Thursday	why

Remember: consonant blends are separate sounds (phonemes) blended together but digraphs and trigraphs are letters which represent just one sound (phoneme).

The National Literacy Strategy materials refer to a *split digraph* which many linguists refer to as a *discontinuous digraph*. This is where the two parts of the digraph are split by an intervening consonant; the effect is to lengthen the preceding vowel, to change it from a short vowel to a long vowel. For example, *mate (/ae/)*, rather than *mat /a/*; *pine (/ie/)*, rather than *pin (/i/)*.

Teachers have long recognised this and have labelled it as the 'magic *e*' rule: 'the *e* at the end of the word makes the other vowel say its name.'

Teachers must now use the *split digraph* terminology to fit in with the National Literacy Strategy games and activities.

The emphasis in National Literacy training materials is on making all of these letter–sound links explicit to children in a very systematic way. You will need to know the appropriate terminology as well as understand some of the pitfalls for young learners. A thorough knowledge of the alphabetic nature of English orthography is essential if we are to understand the problems children may encounter. The NLS (2000) stresses that children need to be proficient in the skills of *segmenting* (breaking down words into their constituent phonemes, for spelling) and *blending* (building words from their constituent phonemes, for reading).

It is believed by some that the segmentation of words into their component phonemes is a relatively simple matter. Segmentation is not, however, as easy as it seems to the adult. The sounds we, and especially young children, pronounce in speech are not always a close match to the actual phonemes. This can be because of the accent of the speaker or because, in rapid speech, sounds often run together. Try saying *'I would like some butter on my sandwich'* at a normal speed. It is probable that many of the phonemes will hardly be apparent at all; depending on your regional accent it could sound more like *'I w'd like s'm bu'er on my sam'idge.'* The task for the young learner in identifying phonemes in words, other than the initial sounds, is huge. As another example, try to identify the number of phonemes in these words: *half, bring, eight, prince, prints, mission, two, tax, necessary, easy.*

If we, as adults who understand the system and generally articulate quite clearly, sometimes have difficulty, it is clear that children's difficulties will be even greater.

Following on from activities which help children develop phonological awareness and begin to identify individual phonemes in words, the next task for children is to learn the written representations of the letters of the alphabet. Classroom resources and displays should include alphabet friezes and posters about letters and words as well as examples of environmental print from supermarkets and advertisements. Similarly, for young children, there needs to be a display which uses the children's names – probably in alphabetical order – because names are usually the first words children become familiar with. Children can often tell you the first letters of their names at a very early age and some can even write these.

There should be name cards, alphabet cards, letters made from a range of materials and materials for children to make letters with, magnet board and magnetic letters, computers with relevant programs (for example, 'Animated Alphabet'), as well as all kinds of writing materials. Letter names and letter sounds should be linked together, so that children realise early on that written letters are the way in which the words/sounds that we speak are recorded on paper.

• Sing songs and rhymes which are rhythmic, alliterative and have clear rhyming words. Sing the Alphabet song 'A, B, C, D...'

• Make up alliterative phrases (Helpful Hassan, Magic Martin, Sleepy Sarah) and ask the children to name the sound/phoneme at the beginning of each word. The children can then make up their own. An extension of this would be to write the phrases on paper or a whiteboard, focusing on the initial phonemes and demonstrating the formation of the letters. Point out the capital letters in names and show the corresponding lower case letters which go with them.

• Use the children's name cards to play games which require children to look at similarities in names and arrange them in sets (same initial letter, same final letter, all those with an /e/ sound in, all those with a particular letter in, all those with the same number of letters/ syllables/phonemes).

• Play 'I Spy' games, focusing on letter sounds and then letter names.

• Make whole-class thematic alphabets with the children (foods, animals, toys, Christmas) which can be illustrated and displayed.

• Seek opportunities to demonstrate writing to the children in shared writing sessions and point out letters which are the same, moving on to identifying the same letter strings/ clusters/spellings of words which sound the same.

• Play games with letters and phonemes using magnetic letters on a magnet board or on large cards, physically combining them to make words.

- Use small wipeable whiteboards for children to write phonemes they can hear in words.

There are a number of phonic games described in the DfEE National Literacy Strategy 'Progression in Phonics': materials for whole-class teaching' (2000) which are interactive and organised under the headings of:
1. hearing and saying
2. identifying phonemes and spelling
3. recognising letters and reading.

More about consonants and vowels

Subject facts

The last section looked at the relationship between the *orthography* (spelling system) of English and its sound system. This section takes a closer look at the working of consonants and vowels.

There is a major difference in the way vowels and consonants are articulated. Vowels are produced by the voice with very little obstruction from the mouth – the mouth and lips are open, sometimes wide as in producing the /a/ sound, sometimes partly closed as in producing the /u/ sound. Consonants are produced with some kind of obstruction from the throat, tongue, teeth or lips. In the previous section you will have noted that there are not just 5 vowels (as in the 26 letter alphabet) but 20 vowel sounds in English.

The letter *y* can be either consonant or vowel, depending on its position in a word; it is known as a *semi-vowel*. You can hear and see the difference by saying words with *y* at the start – *yet, yacht, yes,* where it acts (and is articulated) as other consonants, /y/. Where *y* occurs in the body of the word, as in *sky, my, scythe,* it acts as a vowel, /ie/.

Vowels and consonants in syllables
Vowels are the units of the sound system which usually occupy the middle of a syllable whereas consonants are generally found at the edges of syllables. For example:

> *go* is consonant, vowel – CV
> *on* is vowel, consonant – VC
> *cat* is consonant, vowel, consonant – CVC
> *trip* is consonant, consonant, vowel, consonant – CCVC
> *blue* is consonant, consonant, vowel – CCV

In the phonics progression described by the National Literacy Strategy (2000) materials, work in the earliest stages concentrates on segmenting and blending CVC words, moving on to CCVC words. No words having the other patterns are suggested. The focus on a staged progression (initial consonant, short vowel, final consonant – as in *cat, wet, pig, dog, cup*) in this early work on spelling does not recognise the different rates at which children progress. Clearly children are likely to use vocabulary in their own writing which has other consonant/vowel patterns. If they are using onset/rime and making analogies they will certainly be aware of consonant clusters; many teachers will teach the common initial consonant blends as families of words with the same initial onset blends.

---

bl- bl-ack, bl-ue, bl-ock, bl-ind
br- br-ing, br-ain, br-ead, br-other
dr- dr-aw, dr-ink, dr-eam, dr-ess

See page 28 for more on onset/rime.

Consonant clusters

Consonants can be used singly or combined (blended) with other consonants. Up to three consonants can be used at the beginning of a word in English (as in *string, splash*) and up to five at the end (as in *twelfths*), although these words are rare. Investigation of three-consonant clusters at the beginnings of words will show that they all begin with /s/.

---

sch-	school, scheme
scr-	scream, scramble
shr-	shred, shrimp
spl-	splash, splendid
spr-	spring, spray
str-	strong, stream
scl-	sclerosis (not likely to be found by children)
squ-	squirrel, squash (although the third letter, *u* is not a consonant, *q* is always followed by *u* in English)

Pure vowels and diphthongs

Of the 20 vowel sounds, 12 are classified as *pure vowels*. Five of these are *long vowels* (/ee/, /oo/, /ar/, /ur/, /or/) and seven are *short vowels* (/a/, /e/, /i/, /o/, /u/,/aw/, /er/). This last one is the sound we hear in unstressed syllables in words such as *litter, wooden, circus* and is known as *schwa*.

The remaining eight vowel sounds are all *diphthongs*. A diphthong is a particular kind of vowel digraph. When a diphthong is articulated, the shape of the mouth changes as the sound is made and it is possible to distinguish the two sounds gliding together. Try saying these words and notice what happens:

pain	road	light	down	coin	fear	stairs	cure
/ae/	/oe/	/ie/	/ow/	/oi/	/ear/	/air/	/ue/

Often when children 'sound out' words they are trying to spell which have vowel diphthongs in them, they add additional letters to represent the additional sounds they hear in articulating the word, for example, *roawd (road), coyin (coin)*.

Short vowels and long vowels

In spelling, there are several regular patterns influencing the orthography of vowels.

The short vowels generally become long with the addition of the final *e* (the 'magic *e*' rule which makes the vowel into a long vowel).

hat	hate
then	these
pin	pine
not	note
cut	cute

There are, of course, some frequently used words which are exceptions to this rule, for example, *come, some, love;* in these the vowel sound is not the long */oa/* but the short */u/*. They are examples of words which may have been 'tidied up' by printers, so that they matched the words with the split digraph (see Chapter 4).

Another spelling pattern which marks long from short vowel sounds is the doubled consonant in the middle of a word. Analysis of children's spelling errors shows that it is a frequently encountered hazard. Errors here often produce a word with a different meaning, for example, *later* for *latter, hoping* for *hopping, fury* for *furry, diner* for *dinner*.

Teaching should remind children of the effect of the double letter in shortening the vowel.

The rule that 'the consonant phoneme following a short vowel is represented by a double consonant' is fairly consistent:

marry, carry, yellow, butter, better, rabbit, apple, pillow, sorry.

Why you need to know these facts

The emphasis in the National Literacy Strategy (2000) materials for teaching spelling in the early stages is heavily on children hearing and identifying phonemes and learning regular consonant/vowel patterns. Teachers need a secure background knowledge of both how orthography relates to the sound system and of the terminology required. The vocabulary for describing letters and phonemes needs to be used precisely. Terms like *consonant, vowel, long vowel, short vowel* are used in teachers' materials and increasingly with the children.

Amazing facts

Every word in the English language contains a vowel phoneme! One letter *(y)* can represent either a vowel or a consonant phoneme. Words which have no other vowel have *y* behaving as a vowel. So, *y* in these words (for example, *dry, fly, cry, my, sly, try, shy*) is a vowel phoneme and there is no word without a vowel.

Common misconceptions

It is often said that the English spelling system is chaotic and that it should be reformed to reflect more closely the phonology of the language. This is not really so and it is important to realise that the spelling system of English is not as arbitrary as it may first appear. Once we have some knowledge about how orthography works it becomes clear that there is more regularity than irregularity. Linguists estimate that there are fewer than 500 English words for which the spelling is wholly irregular. It is important for children to be able to make informed predictions about the link between spelling and pronunciation and to understand something of why spellings are as they are.

Teaching ideas

Activities which enable children to link pronunciation with the written word are important. Make sure there are eye-catching/interactive displays highlighting letters and use the terms *consonant* and *vowel*; make sure these are drawn to the children's attention by talking about their content.

• To familiarise the youngest children with the letters of the alphabet, make personal alphabet posters or booklets, using the 'Favourite Things ABC' format:

George's ABC
My favourite things are...
animals
balloons
cats
doughnuts
elephants
fairies
giraffes... etc.

• Carry out shared writing activities using target groups of words:
    – ask children to clap the syllables in the words;
    – point out spelling patterns and the way the letters represent the sounds in the words;
    – ask children to identify the phonemes in the words and the letters which represent them;
    – invite children to look for small words within longer words, for example, the *go* in *going*, the *and* in *hand*.

• Talk explicitly about the split digraphs (for example, *a–e, u–e, i–e*) and focus on what effect the silent *e* has on the preceding vowel. This can be followed with word hunt activities to create class lists of words which have this silent *e* pattern.

• Ask the children to carry out word hunts of all kinds. With younger children, this can be to look for words with particular vowel phonemes or consonant clusters (*oo* words or *tr* blends), and with older children use hunts that could be for particular consonant clusters, including an investigation into three-consonant clusters, to see what pattern emerges.

• Investigate words with *y* in them and classify them according to whether the *y* is a vowel or a consonant.

• Make phoneme cards, consonants and vowels, in sets for particular groups of words and ask children to physically move these around to create the words you suggest. (See NLS (2000) for several examples of this.)

Segmentation – syllables

Syllables can be defined as the beats in a spoken word. Most children do not have difficulty in identifying the number of beats in a word; in fact, clapping the number of beats in each other's names is a frequent activity in Early Years classrooms. For children the task of identifying syllables in spoken language is considerably less challenging than identifying the separate phonemes. Syllables can always be pronounced as separate units and it is for this reason that awareness of syllables generally precedes awareness of phonemes.

Words can be *monosyllabic* (having a single syllable) or *polysyllabic* (having two or more syllables). An open syllable can be a single vowel phoneme *(I, or, ear)* or a vowel preceded by a consonant or consonants *(hear, clear, my, sky, try)*. Closed syllables may start in the same way (with a vowel or with consonants) but these are followed by up to four additional consonants. For example:

an	(vowel + 1 consonant)
ant	(vowel + 2 consonant)
ants	(vowel + 3 consonants)
plant	(2 consonants + vowel + 2 consonants)
plants	(2 consonants + vowel + 3 consonants)

A single syllable can have a large number of consonants but it can have only one vowel. A second vowel would create an extra beat *(plant–er, plant–ing)* and thus two syllables. All syllables must have a vowel phoneme in them.

Dividing words into syllables

The division of written words into syllables often causes disagreement. Although we can offer a definition of a syllable as 'containing a single vowel' with or without consonants preceding or following, division of written polysyllabic words is sometimes open to debate.

For example, although there would not be disagreement about the number of syllables in the word *chimpanzee* (3), it could be divided into its syllables like this: *chim–pan–zee*, or like this: *chimp–an–zee*.

People will generally divide syllables according to whether they favour a phonetic instinct or a grammatical instinct. A word like *handing,* for example, would be divided into two balanced CVC syllables *(han–ding)* by someone following a phonetic instinct, whereas someone following a grammatical instinct would divide it to show the base word + inflectional ending *(hand–ing).*

Often, it does not matter that people may see the syllable boundaries differently. It does matter, however, when long words are hyphenated at the end of a line when there are some rules which should be observed:

- Digraphs (vowel or consonant) should not be split, so *training* could not be split *trai–ning* or *pushing* as *pus–hing.*
- Splits should be made between consonants which could not be a consonant cluster in one syllable, such as *al–ways, on–ly.*
- If a consonant cluster could be attached to either vowel sound, it is attached to the stressed syllable, such as *re–sponse, ex–plain, tickl–ish.*

Stress in polysyllabic words

When a word has more than one syllable, the pronunciation generally gives greater stress to one syllable than others and the stress may not always be on the same group of letters. This is to do with the rhythm and pattern of *stressed* and *unstressed* syllables in English speech, for example, *ap**pear**, **dis**appear, disap**pear**ance.*

The problem of where the stress falls in a word is often one which causes difficulties for those for whom English is a new language and it can sometimes lead to confusion over word meanings, for example, *re**fuse*** (verb) and ***re**fuse* (noun) (rubbish); *in**cline*** (verb) and ***in**cline* (noun) (slope). There is often disagreement between speakers, which eventually gets resolved through usage. A recent example was *controversy* when some insisted that the stress should be on the second syllable as in *con**trov**ersy,* whilst others argued that ***con**troversy* was correct! In the case of the noun/verb distinctions, children (particularly those for whom English is an additional language) would need to be corrected, although where the stress is a matter of debate it would not be necessary.

When a two-syllable word is a *compound word* (a word created from two monosyllabic words), both syllables are equally stressed, for example, *toothbrush , seaside, handbag, teapot.* One way of demonstrating to children the importance of stress in words would be to ask them to experiment with saying some compound words with the stress on the first/the second syllable, to see whether there is a resulting shift of meaning.

Even very young children generally have an innate sense of rhythm so identification of the beats in the language, particularly in words, is a good starting point for analysis. Children enjoy songs and action rhymes with strong rhythmic patterns so best use must be made of this awareness as a starting point for segmenting words and developing insights about syllables. Teachers need to be aware of the characteristics of syllable structure in order to develop the children's knowledge. When thought about the beats/syllables in words moves from the oral to the written forms of words, talk about syllables provides a good context for using vocabulary such as *vowel, consonant, digraph* and for introducing compound words.

Analysing syllables can move smoothly into consideration of onset/rime.

Amazing facts

Long words do not necessarily have more syllables than short words. Sometimes words having the same number of letters have a different number of syllables and short words can sometimes have more syllables than long words. For example:

strength	8 letters/1 syllable
straight	8 letters/1 syllable
elephant	8 letters/3 syllables
open	4 letters/2 syllables

An interesting investigation for older children would be to see who can find the word with the most syllables – it should be a real word, not an invented one!

Teaching ideas

Children find it easier to hear and identify the bigger chunks in words (syllables) rather than individual phonemes. A good starting point with the youngest children is to focus on counting the beats in their names. Games which use this ability can be devised.

• Look at nursery rhymes with predictable and repetitive syllabic patterns, printed on cards, and encourage the children to clap the rhythms of these. This could be extended by helping them pick out the words which have the most beats.

• Write all the children's names on cards and play a sorting game, putting all the names with the same number of syllables into a set. Children could have printed paper versions of the names and cut these up into the syllables. This is a good point to introduce the term *syllable* and to show that each syllable contains a vowel sound.

• Make themed collections of polysyllabic words (for example, foods, animals). Write these down and ask children to divide the written words into their constituent syllables. These written syllables could then be recombined to create new fabulous beasts.

el–e–phant	oct–o–pus	but–ter–fly
el–o–fly	oct–ter–phant	but–e–pus...

• With older children this could lead into discussion about where syllable boundaries lie and the identification of vowels and consonant clusters. This in turn could lead to identification of 'rules' for written syllables.

• Make collections of compound words (two monosyllabic nouns combined to create new words). These can be printed and cut up so that children can experiment with creating their own compound words! Older children could be given an investigative task to find out whether compound words ever have more than two syllables.

• Writing haiku poetry is a productive way of applying knowledge about syllables. A haiku should have seventeen syllables, divided into three lines. The first line should have five syllables, the second should have seven syllables and the third five syllables. Children should be shown examples and invited to count and identify the syllables before they begin work on their own haiku. This activity encourages children to think carefully about both the meaning and the syllable structure of the words they select. It will probably require several attempts before a concise, accurate haiku is achieved.

• Once older children have experimented with writing haiku poems, they could try writing tanka poems. These are a variation of haiku, consisting of 5 lines. The first three lines retain the normal 5, 7, 5 syllable pattern with two additional lines of 7 syllables each.

Segmentation – onset/rime

Subject facts

Children need to move beyond identification of syllables to analysis of the component parts of the syllables. Much recent research (for example, Goswami and Bryant, 1990) has focused on segmentation into *onset* and *rime* rather than into separate phonemes because children find it easier to recognise the onset and rime units in syllables or words. Children who have difficulty identifying the final phoneme in words such as *top* or *tot*, are able to identify those sharing the same rime, such as *hop ,top, stop*. The careful observation of young children carried out by Bradley, Bryant and Goswami (1983, 1993, 1990, 1992), showing just what children could deal with in terms of recognition and analysis, has been very important in guiding teachers. Approaches to phonics teaching which reflect this understanding are often called *new phonics*.

The onset is defined as the consonant phoneme or the consonant cluster before the vowel, and the rime as the vowel and any following consonants.

Onset	Rime
s	ing
st	ing
str	ing
c	at
c	ats
ch	at
ch	ats

A few words and syllables (those which are *open syllables*) have no onsets.

one
or
use
out
aw/ful (first syllable)
in/side (first syllable)

Some two-syllable words, where the second syllable is

unpronounced, are better treated in the same way.

k	ettle
j	umble

In terms of spelling, identification and familiarisation with rime letter patterns can be of great help to learners. The following list (Wylie and Durell, 1970, quoted in Dombey and Moustafa,1998) of thirty-seven rimes, make nearly 500 words.

-ack	-ain	-ake	-ale
-all	-ame	-an	-ank
-ap	-ash	-at	-ate
-aw	-ay	-eat	-ell
-est	-ice	-ick	-ide
-ite	-ill	-in	-ine
-ing	-ink	-ip	-ir
-ock	-oke	-op	-or
-ore	-uck	-ug	-ump
-unk			

Other common rimes include:

-ad	-ag	-age	-ar
-ade	-um(b)	-up	-ot
-amp	-ent	-old	-ust
-een	-ook	-ar	-ew
-ow	-ue	-ut	-ush
-own	-ace	-og	-and
-ift	-ear	-ead	-oon
-oor	-ail	-aid	-end
-ind	-itch	-atch	-oak

Rime analogy

This approach to breaking up words for reading is much more efficient in English than sounding out the separate phonemes in a word. It is also more reliable as a guide for spelling than dependence on simple phonic analysis of words. Once a range of rimes has become familiar, children can make analogies between words; that is, they perceive patterns and are able to draw on this existing knowledge to make sense of new examples. Analogy is a cognitive process which involves recognising the similarity between two things – one of which is familiar and one unfamiliar – and then using knowledge about the familiar to understand the unfamiliar. At the same time, it involves being able to make deductions about the differences between the two items. This can be seen when a young child, familiar with the word *cat* in her reading, is able to see that a new word, *rat*, is like *cat* but has a different letter at the beginning. Using her knowledge of the structure of *cat* and her knowledge of the sound represented by *r*, she is able to make an analogy and to deduce that the new word is *rat*.

Teachers can develop this skill, especially in the early stages, by drawing children's attention to the patterns and pointing out the analogies. If they know the spelling of *name* they can make an analogy with the new words they wish to spell, such as *g–ame, s–ame, fr–ame*. Goswami (1996) has pointed out that there is a much greater spelling-to-sound consistency in English orthography at the onset/rime level than there is at the individual letter/phoneme level. It is also apparent that fluent readers, as well as beginners, make use of onset/rime strategies in that they focus on the largest recognisable visual pattern or 'chunk' rather than on individual components (sounds or phonemes).

Usha Goswami (1995), in her work on the effects of phonological awareness on children's literacy development, suggests that there are three levels or stages of phonological awareness apparent in children's sensitivity to the make-up of words. To begin with they are aware of the following:

syllables	break + fast	din + ner	then
onset and rime	h + and		
	s + and		
	st + and		then
phonemes	h + a + n + d		
	h + e + l + p		
	sh + e + ll		
	t + e + ll		

Usha Goswami states that the sequence shown above is true for all alphabetic languages where studies have been undertaken.

It is important for teachers to understand the basis of onset/rime and to be familiar with the process of analogy so that they are in a position to make the analogies explicit to children. Some children may spontaneously make use of such analogies in their spelling but when they do not, they can be taught to make the links. Traditional phonic approaches use a 'part to whole' approach, teaching individual letters which readers blend into words. Whilst there is some of this approach in the NLS guidance, it is combined with the newer approaches using onset/rime. (See page 33, 'Phonics and Reading/Writing Connections' for more on synthetic (part-to-whole) and analytic (whole-to-part) approaches.)

• Use enlarged texts (big books) of rhymes and poems and, when they are familiar, point out onset/rime in the rhyming words. Use these as starting points for making up more words using the same rime. Good books for this include *Quentin Blake's Alphabet* and his *Mr Magnolia*, and Dr Seuss' *Cat in the Hat* and *The Cat in the Hat Comes Back,* and there are many more rhyming texts which could be used.

• Play a range of 'Odd One Out' games:
  – Orally. Read out a set of words such as *man, can, fan, cup, ran,* and ask children to identify the odd one out. Some of these could be written and split into onset and rime (for example, *m–an*), and children then asked to point out what is the same and what is different in the words.
  – Card games. Make sets of cards with the same rime and add enough odd one out cards for the number of sets. Each child has the first card of the rime set and must build up the complete set of four or five cards by taking cards in turn from a mixed-up box, until a set is complete.

• Make sets of cards with identical pairs of words you wish to focus on and use these to play 'Pairs' or 'Snap'.

• Provide the children with the spelling of a one-syllable word (for example *in*) and ask the children to make new words by adding onsets (for example, *b, t, w, p,* then *ch, sh, th, sp, tw, gr*). When adding the onset, take care not to emphasise the sound (as in *b/er*) but say the complete word, with a slight delay after the first phoneme.

Other complete word rimes which can be used are: *it, at, am, on, an, and, all, ill, ear.* Develop this activity by moving on to rimes which are not words on their own, for example, *-et, -ip, -ell, -ot, -ack.*

• Make posters of the rime sets created by the activity above and display them. As children find more words with the same rimes these can be added to the lists.

• The NLS materials (1998) suggest a useful method for encouraging children to explore the range of words which can be made using onset/rime. Make a set of matrices with onsets (initial consonants and consonant digraphs) provided vertically on the left of the page. Put a selection of rimes horizontally across the top of the page. The rimes can be of varying complexity, depending on the age and needs of the children. The children then try to match the onsets with the rimes to see how many words can be made.

	-at	-all	-ell	-ill	-est	-up
b	bat	ball	bell	bill	best	
c	cat	call	cell			cup
d			dell	dill		
f	fat	fall	fell	fill		
h	hat	hall	hell	hill		
s	sat		sell	sill		sup
t		tall	tell	till	test	
w		wall	well	will	west	
sh			shell			
th	that					
ch	chat			chill	chest	

• Provide sets of magnetic letters and a magnet board so that children can physically move letters around on the board. Give a rime and ask children to make as many words as possible using this rime. This works well as a paired or small group activity. The children should write down each word they make before moving on to another.

Rimes which will produce large numbers of words include: *-at, -ell, -ing, -ame, -ate, -and, -eat, -est, -ar, -ow.* With older children you can use the longer rimes such as: *-itch, -atch, -ight, -ough, -ance, -ain.* This activity helps to reinforce the common letter strings and spelling of the rimes.

Phonics and reading/writing connections

Approaches to the teaching of phonics have always sought to provide children with information about the smallest parts of language – letters, sounds or syllables – as the basis for both reading and writing. It has been assumed that once children have mastered these small parts, they will be able to build them into words for reading and writing. Such approaches are underpinned by a belief that learners move from the parts to the whole. More recently researchers have looked more closely at how children learn about letter–sound relationships and many have come to believe that learners move from knowledge of the whole (knowledge of whole words) to the ability to analyse those words into their constituent parts (letters and sounds). These two different approaches have come to be called *synthetic* (when it is thought that children should learn to synthesize the small items of knowledge to build up words) and *analytic* (where children learn to analyse known whole words and to break them down into their parts).

Reading and writing are taught together in schools but development of reading skills (decoding written language) and writing skills (encoding written language) do not necessarily proceed at the same rate. Indeed there is evidence (Uta Frith, 1985) that progress in one is often ahead of progress in the other. Frith identified three overlapping phases in children's development: logographic, alphabetic and orthographic.

A diagrammatic representation of this, adapted from Frith, is provided by Dombey, Moustafa et al. in *Whole to Part Phonics* (1998) (see Figure 5).

Subject facts

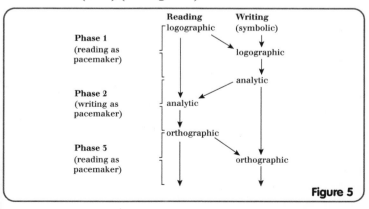

Figure 5

Dombey, Moustafa et al. describe each of the phases as follows:

In Phase 1, reading is ahead of writing. At this stage, the *logographic phase*, in the earliest stages of reading, children recognise and remember words as wholes. They do not pay much attention to the internal structures of words or to the order of the letters, but they recognise whole words.

In Phase 2, writing leads reading. At this stage, the *analytic phase*, children learn to look at and listen to words more closely; they break words down into their constituent parts, match letters and sounds and use this knowledge to write and read unfamiliar words.

In Phase 3, reading once again leads writing. At this stage, the *orthographic phase*, children have become independent readers who are able to recognise many words immediately. They can now also read many unfamiliar words almost instantly, drawing on a growing knowledge of spelling patterns and word structures.

These three phases do not equate to specific ages – they are simply the stages that learners have been observed to move through as they become independent readers and writers.

The significance of this work for the teaching of spelling lies in the recognition that children learn to break words into their parts in the course of learning to write, as they seek ways of representing the sounds they hear in words. Teaching about letter–sound correspondence and individual phonemes is more likely to make sense to learners in the second phase rather than as the starting point for reading. Equally, children's ability to analyse the units within words (onsets/rimes/phonemes), in order to write (spell) them, precedes their ability to use this knowledge in reading.

This research suggests that children generally use phonic knowledge first to break down words into the sounds they can hear, before they learn how to build them up – in other words their approaches are analytic rather than synthetic. Whether children are able to make sense of synthetic phonics teaching will depend upon their Nursery and pre-school experiences of the written language of stories and rhymes and of playing with words and letters. They need to have heard many stories and rhymes read aloud, and to have both read and made alphabet books. They also need to have seen teachers writing in shared writing sessions and scribing individual children's words, as well as having a large repertoire of rhymes and songs. As Dombey, Moustafa et al. (1998) say:

Whole-to-part phonics instruction differs from traditional phonics instruction in that:

i) it teaches parts of the words after a story has been read to, with and by children rather than before the story is read by children, and

ii) it teaches letter–onset, letter–rime and letter–syllable correspondences rather than letter–phoneme correspondences. Yet, like traditional phonics instruction, it is explicit, systematic and extensive.

Why you need to know these facts

The National Literacy Strategy Framework for Teaching, in the earliest stages, is very clear that the work which children do at word level should arise from the texts (stories, rhymes, and so on) used in the whole-class shared reading or writing sessions. In other words the children should be familiar with the words in texts before they are asked to consider the constituent parts. 'Shared reading provides a context for applying and teaching word level skills...' (NLS Framework p.11). The 'Progression in Phonics' materials, although apparently separate, can also be implemented within the context of the reading texts selected. Teachers need to be aware that children will make more sense of instruction about the constituent parts of words if they have a context for this work and are familiar with the words they are working with.

Teaching ideas

• Shared reading provides a good context for work on individual words. Once the children are familiar with a text you can:

– Use Post-it Notes or pieces of card attached with Blu-Tack to cover rhyming words and ask the children to provide the rhymes.

– Use Post-it Notes or pieces of card attached with Blu-Tack to cover onsets or rimes of words and ask the children to spell the missing parts. When volunteers have had a try, the covers can be peeled off to check their attempts.

– Use Post-it Notes or pieces of card attached with Blu-Tack to cover inflectional endings (for example, verb endings *-ing* or *-ed* or plurals) and ask children what should be there. (See page 65 for more on inflectional endings.)

- Ask children to divide selected words into onset/rime and then to provide more words with the same rime. Write these on a flip chart so that children can see the letter strings in the rimes.

- Use texts which contain a proportion of the words on the NLS high-frequency or medium-frequency word lists (NLS Framework for Teaching, pages 60–3); cover these words and ask children to write them with correct spelling on personal whiteboards. This can be a paired activity at first. Check by looking back at the shared text.

- Teach children the Look, Say, Cover, Write, Check strategy (see pages 50–1) and apply this to teaching new words. For example, if specific vocabulary is used in a new book or in another subject, such as history, write selected words on a flip chart and ask children to look carefully and try to memorise the spelling before flipping the page over and asking children to write the new word from memory. Flip the page back to allow them to check. Several sessions on the same words will often be needed.

- In shared writing sessions ask children to provide the spelling of parts of words or whole words. This is especially helpful to reinforce new spellings and also to check which children can spell particular words.

Resources

References and further reading

Bradley, L and Bryant, P (1983) 'Categorising sounds and learning to read: a causal connection' *Nature* 301 pp 419–21

Bryant, P (1993) 'Phonological Aspects of Learning to Read' in Beard, R (ed) *Teaching Literacy, Balancing Perspectives*, London: Hodder and Stoughton

Crystal, D (1995) *The Cambridge Encyclopedia of the English Language*, Cambridge: Cambridge University Press

DfEE (1998) *National Literacy Strategy Framework for Teaching*, London: DfEE

DfEE (2000) *National Literacy Strategy. 'Progression in Phonics: materials for whole-class teaching'*, London: DfEE

Dombey, H & Moustafa, M (1998) *Whole to Part Phonics*, London: CLPE

Frith, U (1985) 'Developmental dyslexia' in Patterson, KE et al. (eds) *Surface Dyslexia*, Hove: Lawrence Erlbaum

Associates Ltd
Gentry, D (1982) 'An analysis of developmental spelling in
GNYS AT WRK' in *The Reading Teacher*, Vol. 36(2)
Goswami, U and Bryant, P (1990) *Phonological Skills and
Learning to Read*, Hove: Lawrence Erlbaum Associates Ltd
Goswami, U (1992) *Analogical Reasoning in Children*, Hove:
Lawrence Erlbaum Associates Ltd
Goswami, U (1995) 'Phonological development and reading
by analogy: what is analogy and what is not?' in *Journal of
Research in Reading*, Vol. 18 Issue 2, 1995
Goswami,U (1996) 'Rhyme and Analogy' in *Child Education*,
May pp 28–9

Classroom resources
Big Book versions of children's stories and non-fiction texts,
for shared reading. Many publishers now produce these,
together with standard sized versions for individual or
group reading.
Alphabet Books and early dictionaries, large and small.
Big book stand, designed to hold a large book open so that
all children can see the text.
Easel and paper or flip charts and pens for whole-class
sessions and shared writing.
Alphabet posters. Provide changing displays of these so that
they are noticed and can be used for reference when
children are writing.
Magnet boards and magnetic letters, for use in teaching and
also for children's own use.
Nursery Rhyme Books – both big books and standard sized
versions.
Books of finger rhymes and songs for teacher reference. A
classic collection is Elizabeth Matterson (ed) (reprinted
1991) *This Little Puffin* (Puffin Books), but there are many
collections from different publishers.
Individual whiteboards and markers for use in whole-class
and group sessions – at least enough for children to work in
pairs.

ICT resources
Computer programs such as:
The Animated Alphabet
My Oxford Word Box (Oxford University Press)
Nursery Rhyme Time (Sherston Software)
Oxford Reading Tree Rhyme and Analogy (Sherston
Software)
Dr Seuss' ABC (Living Books)

Chapter 2
Spelling development

Sentences

This chapter looks at aspects of what is known about children's spelling development and at strategies which are effective in learning and teaching how to spell.

During the last twenty or so years, much has been learned about children's spelling development. It is important for teachers to have some knowledge about the stages of development that are apparent in the spelling of a majority of children as they move towards conventional forms. This is not to suggest that all children will move through all stages or that development *will* happen without some teaching. Nor is it true that each of the identified stages will be separate and discrete; there is often evidence of several strategies being used at the same time. However, knowledge which enables teachers to analyse a child's errors and strategies will indicate what kind of intervention and teaching might be needed at a specific point.

There is also now more awareness of the links between handwriting and spelling. Research into children's spelling development has recently focused on the part handwriting plays in helping children to spell words correctly. It has been suggested that spelling is learned 'as much in the hand as in the eye'. Although opinion is divided about the stage at which children should be taught a cursive (joined) script, a growing number of schools are teaching joined writing from the start. The arguments for doing this, to help children's spelling, are strong, though teachers will need to follow the agreed policy of the school in which they teach.

There is a greater understanding of the need to *teach* children how to learn spellings. It is not enough to provide lists of words to be learned and subsequently tested; we need to show children how to look closely at words and to develop their visual memories if we are to help them become accurate spellers.

The use of dictionaries also has to be taught. Knowledge of how dictionaries are organised and what information can be found in them is essential as children get older. An interest in word meanings and their history can contribute to children's growth as spellers as well as developing their vocabulary.

Stages of spelling development

A number of researchers have looked closely at young children's spelling development and at the strategies the children use in trying to write (spell) words. In particular, important work was carried out by Gentry (1982) looking at children's independent writing, which enabled him to identify five main stages of development. Other researchers used slightly different labels for the stages, but the process of development was the same. Gentry defined the stages as follows.

Subject facts

1. Pre-communicative

Pre-communicative

Figure 1

The child:
- writes purposefully with the intention to communicate;
- demonstrates some knowledge of the alphabet by forming letters to represent a message;
- has no knowledge of letter–sound correspondence;
- is uncertain of directionality (for example, left to right in English);
- may mix numbers and letters, upper and lower case letters;
- may invent letter-like symbols.

2. Semi-phonetic

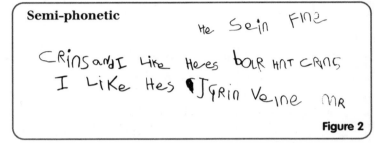

Semi-phonetic

Figure 2

The child:
- begins to match letters to sounds in words;
- abbreviates words – one or two letters represent a whole word;
- often uses letter–name strategies (for example, R = *are*);
- is beginning to grasp left to right directionality;
- shows a growing knowledge of the alphabet and the formation of letters;
- may understand and use word separation/word boundaries.

3. Phonetic

Phonetic

tis   si   my GRANY

Hos   and itis si   moNTNT

ty   RT SLEB   aND

IT,   is   dRk and

my   GRANY   Hom is

Nis

Figure 3

The child:

- now understands that words are represented by letters and works hard to represent each phoneme he or she can hear;
- vowel phonemes are often omitted;
- is systematically using particular (though not always correct) spellings for details of phonetic forms (for example, *ed, nd*);
- often uses unconventional letter sequences;
- assigns letters strictly on the basis of sound;
- usually shows understanding of word separation and spatial orientation.

4. Transitional

Transitional

A Pricess in the Army
A few yeas ago there was a pricess who wanted to joun the army But her perantes woud not let her. She had an elda brother who said you cant joun the army yare a girle. you male shovanest pig she said. At last there perants gave up. all right they said you can joun the army The next day she pased her bags and went to joun the army. The rejamant she jouned was the paris.

Figure 4

The child:

- adheres to the basic tradition of the English spelling system;
- uses vowels/vowel digraphs in every syllable;
- may reverse some letters in words as visual strategies develop (for example, *siad* for *said*);
- uses a growing range of correctly spelled words.

5. Correct

Correct

It's a hot day and weve Just had a probelom.
It's been sorted out now But I will tell you
It all Started yesterday when paul, Susan, and Sheridan had Just come back from the mill.
we went into the girls bedroom and then into the frontroom we heard a noise from upstairs, paul said it's a ghost and laughed, But then a man came down the stairs

Figure 5

The child:
- now consistently spells the majority of words correctly or nearly correctly;
- has a knowledge of word structure (for example, prefixes and suffixes);
- is able to distinguish homonyms;
- shows growing accuracy in the use of silent and double consonants;
- tries out possible spellings and uses visual knowledge to select the correct form;
- has a large spelling vocabulary of learned words;
- continues to master uncommon patterns and irregular spellings, using visual memory.

At the *Phonetic Stage*, it is important to be aware that over-correction can undermine children's confidence as writers and that teaching needs to move children beyond using just phonic strategies to *looking* closely at the letters in words.

At the *Transitional Stage*, direct teaching about the structure of words, letter strings and patterns in words can be particularly helpful.

Why you need to know these facts

Throughout the process of development, it is essential that teaching about spelling is provided. Your ability as teacher to recognise a child's current misconceptions will impact upon the content of that teaching at a particular point. The NLS materials for Key Stage 1 focus on teaching children about phonemes and letter–sound correspondences, whilst the new Key Stage 2 Spelling Bank (2000) focuses on letter patterns and rules.

Amazing facts

The spelling errors of beginner writers are rarely illogical. Careful analysis of errors usually reveals the child's current hypotheses about how the system works. The terms *invented spelling* or *creative spelling* have been used to describe early spelling and these terms reflect the fact that considerable thought underpins what young writers do. In the view of Ferriero and Teberosky (1979), 'writing is a conceptual task, as well as a psycho-motor task' and development 'is not passive copying but active interpretations of the models of the adult world'.

It is interesting to note that children using other languages, some of which are phonically more regular than English, also move through a series of hypotheses as they learn about the system – Ferriero and Teberosky's research was carried out in Buenos Aries!

- **At Stage 2**
  – Work with rhymes and songs to develop phonological awareness.
  – Play 'I Spy' games, focusing on the initial sounds of words.
  – Use children's names as starting points for alliterative alphabets (see Chapter 1).
  – Work on learning the letters of the alphabet, using a wide range of resources.
  – Carry out lots of writing so that the children can see it; talk about the direction of the writing, what to do when you reach the end of a line, the letters you are writing; use vocabulary such as *letter, word, line, space.*
  – Encourage the children to write messages for all kinds of purposes and to experiment with writing.

- **At Stage 2**
  – Continue with all the activities for Stage 1.
  – Demonstrate and talk constantly about letter graphemes and sounds.
  – Play games with letters on cards, combining these to make simple CVC words.
  – Demonstrate the spelling of a bank of familiar words and use these constantly.
  – Encourage children to dictate their texts and let them watch you writing.
  – Show how words can be changed by adding different onsets to rimes – magnetic boards and letters are particularly good for this.

- **At Stage 3**
  – Continue with regular shared writing, to demonstrate spellings.
  – Continue working with onset and rimes and encourage the use of analogy for learning the spelling of words which are like those they already know.
  – Teach regular letter strings such as *-ed, -ing, -and.*
  – Set up and use computer software such as *The Animated Alphabet* as well as word processing programs.
  – Use the games and activities suggested in the NLS *Progression in Phonics* (1999) materials.
  – Teach the Look, Say, Cover, Write, Check routine.

- **At Stage 4**
  – Continue with Stage 3 activities, extending the range of common letter strings/spelling patterns.

– Make collections of words with the same rime, the same initial blends (*st-, str-, br-, bl-,* and so on), the same consonant and vowel digraphs (*th-, ch-, sh-, ea, ow,* and so on) and make wall displays of these.
– Make and use cards for words with common letter patterns, to play 'Pelmanism' ('Pairs') or 'Snap'.
– Investigate and make collections of words with different letter patterns which represent the same sound *(tree, meat, be, key)*.

- **At Stage 5**
– Select activities from all the above to teach and reinforce particular spellings when intervention seems to be needed.
– Teach spelling rules which are reliable (the split digraph/'magic *e*', double consonants, inflectional endings) (see pages 16, 21 and 65).
– Teach about prefixes and suffixes (see pages 68–75) and other elements of word structure.
– Create word webs for families of words (see page 78).
At this point it is important to sustain and develop children's interest in words, word structure, spelling patterns and the history of words to help them master new spellings and to increase their vocabulary.

Spelling – handwriting connections

Subject facts

Traditionally, handwriting teaching has started with teaching the youngest children to form individual letters, moving on to *printing* whole words (see Figure 6).

a b c d e f g h i j k l m

Figure 6

Once this is established, usually at about seven years, children are then taught cursive or joined writing (see Figure 7).

abcdefghijklmn
opqrstuvwxyz

Figure 7

Stage Three, joined where appropriate only
Jarman, 1982

In fact many children regard doing joined writing as a milestone and may experiment with it before they are taught because it is symbolic of being grown up. It is generally agreed that the ability to write swiftly and legibly is essential in developing correct spelling and that teaching the correct formation of letters from an early stage is important. If you reflect on your own writing you may recall having realised that you had made an error in writing a word quickly because the hand movement had not felt right. It is certainly true that there is, in older children, a correlation between swift, clear handwriting and spelling ability.

Margaret Peters (1985) suggests that serious consideration should be given to whether children should be taught joined writing from the beginning of a child's school life.

She lists the advantages as:

1. There is no change 'from print to cursive' in the junior years. Hence, there is never any question of 'low status' as there is in children who have not started joined writing.
2. Words are separate from the beginning and the concept of 'a word' is acquired from the time a child begins to write.
3. Correct letter formation is ensured from the beginning. Too many children just 'pick up' joined writing in the junior years with little help in the conventional letter formation that is crucial to legibility.
4. Spelling is helped, since letter strings are necessarily connected – ame, ough per, *etc.*

Peters, 1985 (page56)

Others have picked up and promoted this idea, notably Cripps and Cox (1990). They believe that children should be taught joined writing on entry to school because this will improve their spelling. They provide a list of advantages very similar to Peters' and also describe the disadvantages of print script.

• *Print script does not follow on from the free scribble movements that children make when they first hold a pencil. These can, however, be developed into a 'running writing' style.*
• *With print script, children break a natural sequence of development by learning disconnected forms and cramped movements. Later, they have another break*

*when they have to learn joined writing. Many also revert
to the disconnected letters that they first learned at
school...*
* *Because print script letters do not join, children do not
learn how to space letters. (In cursive writing, the joining
stroke makes a natural space between two letters.) ...*
* *With print script concentration on letter formation
prevents the word from flowing from the end of the pen...*

Cripps and Cox, 1990

Other handwriting experts do not entirely agree with Peters
and Cripps and Cox. Sassoon (1990) is not convinced by the
idea of joined writing helping spelling and she has doubts
about five-year-olds having the co-ordination skills to
achieve continuous joined writing. She does, however,
suggest that when using print script children should be
taught to include an exit stroke on letters which finish on
the baseline.

Figure 8

Jarman, 1982

She also favours the use of common letter sequences when
children are joining letters to familiarise young writers with
these, though she warns against combining handwriting
with phonics teaching (Sassoon, 1990). Cripps and Cox (op.
cit.) also recommend the use of letter names and not the
sounds when teaching handwriting.

Many LEAs have implemented the teaching of joined
writing from the time children start school and there is a
feeling that this is improving children's handwriting.

The vocabulary for teaching handwriting and the related
concepts should also be taught to children as they get older.
Sassoon advocates using consistent terminology throughout
the school; Cripps and Cox suggest these terms would
include: *'top, bottom, up, down, round, over, back, letter,
word, pattern, left, right, join, curved, straight, tall, short,
long, horizontal, diagonal.'* To these we should add
ascenders and *descenders* as in National Curriculum
requirements.

The National Literacy Strategy Framework includes
Handwriting in the Word Level requirements for Key Stage

1 in considerable detail and with a prescribed progression. In Year 1 pupils should be taught:

> *to practise handwriting in conjunction with spelling and independent writing, ensuring correct letter orientation, formation and proportion, in a style that makes the letters easy to join later.*

In Years 2 and 3 there are prescribed pairs of letters to be practised using the 'four basic handwriting joins'. The vocabulary includes *horizontal, diagonal and ascenders.* It is interesting that there is no guidance on the groupings of individual letters to be taught in the early stages, even though most handwriting experts (for example, Cripps and Cox, and Sassoon) do suggest a sequence based on the way in which letters are formed rather than on alphabetical order. Sassoon's order is:

> *i, l, t, u, y, j – all downward strokes/downward strokes with a 'swing';*
> *r, n, m, h, b, p, k – down strokes followed by a 'bridge';*
> *c, a, d, g, q, o, e – anti-clockwise curves;*
> *v, w, x, z – diagonally straight lines;*
> *s and f – not in any group.*

Many teachers will start with the letters in the child's name.

Some schools adopt published handwriting schemes in which the letters to be taught are grouped in a similar way and progression is built into the scheme.

The specific teaching of handwriting is included in word level work in the National Literacy Strategy so it is important to understand its place in the literacy curriculum. The National Curriculum documentation (2000) gives general guidance but very little detail about what should be taught, though the Key Stage 1 Programme of Study does imply that joined writing should be taught before the junior years:

> *Handwriting*
> *In order to develop a legible style, pupils should be taught:*
> *g how to join letters.*

National Curriculum English (page 49)

Why you need to know these facts

In Key Stage 2 both print and joined writing are required:

Handwriting and presentation
Pupils should be taught to:
a write legibly in both joined and printed styles with increasing fluency and speed
b use different forms of handwriting for different purposes.

National Curriculum English (page 57)

The arguments presented by Peters and Cripps and Cox about the role handwriting plays in spelling are strong and this influence appears to be reflected in National Curriculum requirements.

Common misconceptions

Teachers sometimes believe that slow writers make fewer spelling errors because they are looking carefully at the letters in words. Fast writers are often seen as careless when in fact the opposite is true. Research has shown that the slow writer is often one who is uncertain of letter formation and is faced with a decision every time he or she comes to a fresh letter. Frequently he or she makes a random attempt at the letter he or she is writing. The swift writer is one who is certain of letter formation and is also certain of letter sequences so that a reasonable attempt can be made at a word he or she may never have written before. Careful spellers are generally the faster writers.

Teaching ideas

• Provide a range of materials for children to make letters (play dough, Plasticine, clay) and also to trace out the letter shapes (in sand trays, sticky paint).

• Handwriting teaching is better carried out in small groups (perhaps in a guided group session in the Literacy Hour) so that you can check on pen/pencil grip (and intervene when necessary) and on letter formation.

• Whether teaching is done with a group or with the whole class, children should be seated so that they can see your demonstrations without having to twist round because they are seated around tables. Short, frequent practice sessions appear to work best.

• Letters should be taught in groups sharing similar characteristics of formation and should be taught with an exit stroke to make joining easier.

• Once letters are being joined, use the letter strings/ spelling patterns which are the focus of other teaching in the literacy sessions.

• Combine teaching common letter patterns/word families/prefixes/suffixes and so on with handwriting practice by asking children to make charts or displays of the work they have done (for example, word webs), concentrating on the presentation and handwriting in the display.

Memory and how to learn a spelling

In order to become good spellers children need to develop a good visual memory. It is in this area that direct teaching about *how* to learn a spelling is essential.

Subject facts

It is important to remember that learning is an active task and that we have to think about how we can remember something. We also remember things better if we already know something about them – if we have existing knowledge to which we can attach new knowledge. Memory works by building links. It is difficult to remember things we do not understand but we do remember unusual things and things which interest us. If new information is organised into groups, patterns or categories, it is easier to remember.

There are clear implications for the teaching of spelling in these understandings about memory and remembering.

1. Groups of words having similar patterns will more easily be remembered than lists of unconnected words.
2. Making explicit links between known words, patterns and letter strings and new spellings will make the connections easier to see and understand.
3. Explaining the reasons for a particular spelling pattern, or giving such rules as are reliable will help the learner to remember.
4. It is important to develop children's interest in words.

As has been stated (see Chapter 1), the 'sounding out' of words is not a reliable way to work out the spelling except for simple CVC words. Children must move from dependence on a sounding strategy to looking closely at words.

Even weak spellers can be taught to spell correctly if they are helped to look at words closely and intently. You need to direct the child's attention to the significant parts of the word, whether that is the structure of the word (for example, *un + happy / unhappy, talk + ing / talking*), words hidden within a word (for example, the *moth* in *Timothy*, the *die* in *soldier,* the *ear* in *hear* and *heard,* the *hat* in *what*) or the hard spot in the word (for example, *Wednesday* – note the *nes* in the middle, *parliament* – remember *ia* in the middle).

'Looking with intent' is the phrase used by Margaret Peters (1985) to describe what learners need to do in order to learn words. The aim is to internalise the pattern of the letters in the word with the intention of reproducing it. Children must learn to focus on the meaning and/or the letter strings, to create a visual image of the word. As children become more familiar with the orthography of English and begin to realise that certain letter strings are improbable whilst others are likely, then they will begin to assess the probability of certain graphemes appearing together.

A young child, using phonic analysis, can produce *hogz* for *hugs, jrems* for *dreams, skwek* for *squeak, perfikt* for *perfect* (all genuine examples) because they are unaware the letter combinations *(gz , jr, skw, kt)* are not used in English.

The focus on 'looking with intent' led to the development of the Look, Say, Cover, Write, Check routine for learning a new word.

> 1. *LOOK at the word carefully and in such a way that you will remember what you have seen.*
> 2. *COVER the word so that you cannot see it.*
> 3. *WRITE the word from memory, saying it softly to yourself as you are writing.*
> 4. *CHECK what you have written. If you have not written the word correctly, do not alter it, instead go back and repeat all these steps again.*
>
> *Peters, 1967 (page 66)*

This basic routine has been extended by others, to include fuller guidance on how to help yourself learn.

Torbe (1995) provides the following *aide mémoire.*

How to help yourself to spell

LOOK

Look at the word; say it to yourself.
If you have difficulties remembering how to
write it, trace it with your finger.
See if it looks the way it sounds.
Mark the bit of the word that causes you
difficulties.

COVER

Shut your eyes: see if you can see the word in
your head. Do this for at least 13 seconds.
If you can't see it in your head, say the word to
yourself and see if the sound reminds you of
how it looks.

REMEMBER *If that doesn't work, look again at the word*
and say it in a way that will remind you of how
it is spelled. Exaggerate it. Pronounce the bits
separately – but remember how it is spelled.

WRITE

Cover the word: write it from memory. Try to
see the word in your head as you write.
If you're not sure about it look at it again

CHECK

Check back to see if you got it right.
If you didn't, do it again.
Later in the day, write it again from memory.
If you're not sure of it, look it up before you try.

This advice, directed at children, is much more specific and
helpful, especially the last part about rewriting the word from
memory later in the day. It has been suggested that, after a
period of learning, recall rises for a short while (about 10
minutes) and then falls steeply (80% of detail is forgotten
after 24 hours). It is possible to 'fix' the new learning by
reviewing what has been learned. With a proper review after
10 minutes, then within 24 hours, again within a week and at
intervals after that, recall can be maintained long term.

This suggests that it is important to revisit newly learned
spellings frequently to start with if they are to remain
permanently in the memory. It is essential for learners to
experience success so practice like this needs to be short
and frequent. Torbe (1995) suggests that six- to eight-year-
olds can cope with three simple words daily, nine- to
eleven-year-olds with four words and eleven- to fourteen-
year-olds with six.

Spelling development

It is important to know about factors which will help or hinder children's learning. As well as teaching a routine for learning new words, it helps to explain to older children the reasons for a particular approach. Most children are interested in why they remember or forget things. A learning strategy such as this makes explicit to children the connections between the look and the sound of a word and also promotes development of visual memory. The ultimate aim is to enable children to solve spelling problems independently and not to rely on you.

Amazing facts

Spoken language has no spelling; the correct spelling of a word does not exist until that word is written! The spelling of any word is as it is only because literate people have agreed that this should be so. We do not have to spell correctly in order to talk articulately and fluently. Children who talk confidently have to master a new range of skills in order to write as fluently and confidently.

Common misconceptions

It is commonly believed that the way to improve spelling is to read more. In fact, reading and writing/spelling are two different processes. Efficient readers do not pay attention to the structure or detail of written words except when they encounter a completely unknown word. Writers, on the other hand, must pay careful attention to the structure and graphic representation of what they wish to spell. Many avid and competent readers are poor spellers and, conversely, there are many people who read very little who are very good spellers.

Teaching ideas

• Teach the Look, Cover, Remember, Write, Check routine to the whole class, using vocabulary which the children will need to use.

• Teach together sets of words which have the same spelling pattern whether or not they have the same sounds, for example, *'said, paid, laid, raid'*; *'hear, dear, bear, fear'*; *'our, your, four, hour'*.

• Play 'Shannon's Game'. This is like 'Hangman', but the letters must be produced in the correct order to encourage prediction of letter strings. Use a chalkboard, whiteboard or flip chart and write a number of dashes for letters; you can provide the first letter for young children:

> b _ _ _ _
> Players will probably suggest a vowel next or certain consonants (*l, r*).
>   b r _ _ _
> A vowel will probably be suggested next.
>   b r i _ _
> Given that this is a five-letter word, the options for the next letter are still quite wide: (*b, c, d, e, n, s*).
>   b r i n _
> But once the *n* is in place, the prediction of *g* is highly likely.
>   b r i n g

Keep a tally of the number of guesses and give the next letter if impossible combinations are being suggested. Commentary on the children's suggestions will help their thinking, especially if you point out where guesses appear random. The choice of word can be tailored to the age and needs of the children as well as to particular letter patterns you wish to reinforce.

• With young children, play 'Kim's Game' or 'Pelmanism' to encourage careful looking at objects and letters.

• Create word chains, where the final letter of the first word given must be the first letter of a new word:

> happy / yes / school / look / kettle / elephant / train / number / rhythm…

The difficulty of this can be increased by calling for the last two letters to be at the beginning of the new word.

• Ask children to find the small words in longer ones. It is important to stress that the words must exist in the longer word. Letters cannot be used randomly because the aim is to reinforce the letter patterns:

island	–	is, land, and, an, a
another	–	a, an, no, not, her, the, he, other
grandmother	–	grand, and, moth, mother, other, the, her, he, a, an

Dictionary strategies

Learning to use a *dictionary* and, later, a *thesaurus* is an essential aid to spelling. Apart from its use as a meaning and spelling check, the dictionary is also a source of information about pronunciation and the roots or history of words.

A short history

We use dictionaries to find out about the *lexicon* of English. The term *lexicon* was in use as early as the 17th century and meant 'a book containing a selection of the words in the language with their meanings, arranged in alphabetical order'. The term comes from the Greek *lexis* meaning *word*. Someone who records and defines the vocabulary, word formation, development and history of the language in a dictionary is a *lexicographer*.

The first true lexicographer was Dr Samuel Johnson who completed *A Dictionary of the English Language* in 1755 (see Appendix). Over a seven-year period he compiled a dictionary of definitions of about 40,000 words and he is credited with having 'conferred stability' on the language. It is to Johnson that we owe very many of the accepted spellings in English. A few of his definitions were rather idiosyncratic. The famous ones include:

> Oats: *a grain, which in England is generally given to horses, but in Scotland supports the people.*
> Lexicographer: *a writer of dictionaries; a harmless drudge, that busies himself in tracing the original, and detailing the signification of words.*

Prior to this dictionary there had been others, notably Richard Mulcaster (1580s) (see Appendix) and Nathaniel Bailey (1721), who had attempted to suggest some standardisation and offer definitions. Bailey's dictionary had more entries than Johnson's but lacked illustrative examples and was really only a spelling dictionary.

After Johnson's authoritative work there was no further development of dictionary projects until the genesis of the *Oxford English Dictionary* (OED) in 1879, under the editorship of James AH Murray. The growth of this took many years, with the final section appearing in 1928, long after Murray's death. Supplements to this were published from 1933 and work goes on continuously. The latest

revision was published in 20 volumes in 1989, with a
CD-ROM version. A new edition is planned for 2005.

It is the OED which has become the authoritative version
of the English dictionary and many of the 'Concise',
'Shorter' and 'Children's' editions are derived from it,
though there are other reputable publishers (especially
Collins, Chambers) who also publish dictionaries, including
children's editions, some of which are illustrated.

Learning to use a dictionary

The first requirement for being able to use a dictionary is
knowledge of *alphabetical order*. Young children should be
helped to learn this order as soon as possible through such
activities as:
* making themed alphabet books;
* using class registers and address books;
* showing how indexes work in books.

Once the order is known, show children how to put lists of
items into alphabetical order,
starting with a list of words all beginning with different
letters: *school, book, garden, dog, toys, mummy, fish, water.*

Teach children how to go through the alphabet in their
heads and to look for words beginning with each letter.
Explain that there will not necessarily be a word for each
letter: *book, dog, fish, garden, mummy, school, toys, water.*

Once children can do this, move on to using second, third
and subsequent letters in the word: *bath, bird, bed, baby,
ball, bread, book.*

All these words begin with *b* so the next letter must be
used to get the order: *bath, baby, ball.* All begin with *b*
followed by *a,* so we have to look at the third letter in order
to put them in order: *baby, ball, bath.*

Next, look to see which second letter comes after *a: bed,*
so that comes next. Continue with each of the second letters
to complete the order: *baby, ball, bath, bed, bird, book,
bread.*

Once children have learned to look at letter order in
individual words, show them how the dictionary can be
divided into *quartiles* so making location of letter sections
easier:

```
         ABCDEF          MNOPQR
         GHIJKL          STUVWXYZ
```

After practice at finding the right quartile for a particular letter, introduce children to *headwords* in dictionaries, showing how to use them to help locate individual words, so that they do not look through all the words in one letter section to find a word.

Show how the headwords are used to show which word appears at the start of the page and which at the end. For example, page 450 of the *Concise Oxford Dictionary* (1982 edition) has these headwords:

halfpenny	ham

Explain to children that any word beginning with the letters between *half-* and *ham-* will be on this page; this includes *hali-, hall-, halm-, halo-, halt-, halv- ,haly-, ham-*. This concept needs to be demonstrated to children in order that words can be found more quickly when they are using dictionaries.

Some simple children's dictionaries do not use headwords, but instead use the first two or three letters of listed words as headings. The Oxford *Spell it Yourself* (1992) dictionary uses this system. For example, page 50 has the headings:

je	ji	jo	ju

Page 82 has the headings:

she	shi	sho	shr

As each of these aspects of dictionary *organisation* is taught to them, children will need to carry out lots of activities which will enable them to practise using the information they have learned.

Reading the information

Children also need to be taught how to read the information that is given in the dictionary about a word.

Often abbreviations will be used both to explain the grammatical function of a word and its derivation/history *(etymology)*.

From *The Concise Oxford Dictionary* (2001, OUP)

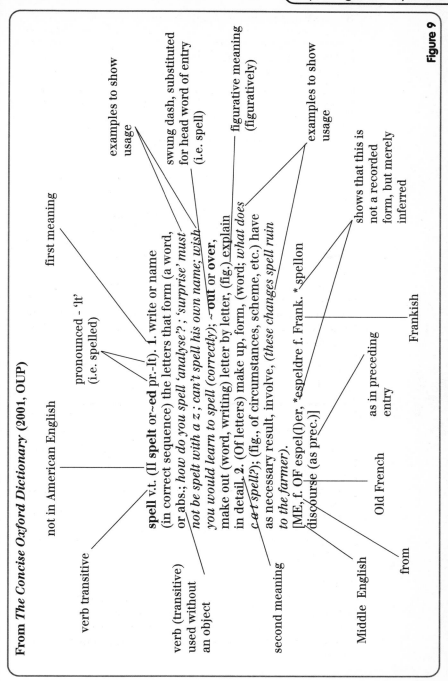

verb transitive

verb (transitive) used without an object

second meaning

Middle English

Old French

from

first meaning

pronounced - 'lt' (i.e. spelled)

not in American English

Frankish

as in preceding entry

shows that this is not a recorded form, but merely inferred

examples to show usage

swung dash, substituted for head word of entry (i.e. spell)

figurative meaning (figuratively)

examples to show usage

spell v.t. (II **spelt** or~**ed** pr.-lt). **1.** write or name (in correct sequence) the letters that form (a word, or abs.; *how do you spell 'analyse'?*; *'surprise' must not be spelt with a z*; *can't spell his own name*; *wish you would learn to spell (correctly)*; ~ **out** or **over,** make out (word, writing) letter by letter, (fig.) explain in detail. **2.** (Of letters) make up, form, (word; *what does c-a-t spell?*); (fig., of circumstances, scheme, etc.) have as necessary result, involve, (*these changes spell ruin to the farmer*). [ME, f. OF espel(l)er, *espeldre f. Frank. * spellon discourse (as prec.)]

Figure 9

POCKET GUIDES: SPELLING AND VOCABULARY   57

Some standard abbreviations are:

Word classes/parts		Etymology (examples)	
n.	noun	AF.	Anglo-French
vb.	verb	Celt.	Celtic
a.	adjective	F.	French
adv.	adverb	Gk.	Greek
prep.	preposition	Ind.	of the subcontinent
conj.	conjunction	L.	Latin
pron.	pronoun	ME	Middle English
pref.	prefix	OE	Old English
suf.	suffix	OF	Old French
s.	singular	ON	Old Norse
pl.	plural	OS	Old Saxon
compar.	comparative	O Celt.	Old Celtic
superl.	superlative	WS	West Saxon

This is only a small sample of the abbreviations which are used in dictionaries, but they are the abbreviations most likely to be encountered in shorter dictionaries. All abbreviations used in any particular dictionary are given by that publisher, so unfamiliar ones can be checked.

Why you need to know these facts

It is often believed that writers would generally spell better if they made more use of dictionaries. Although there are now many more simple/children's dictionaries which are more accessible to children, using a dictionary is not a simple matter. In fact, over-simplification can be misleading because the range of meanings offered is limited. Young writers need to be taught how to use a dictionary or a thesaurus efficiently, so teachers need to understand the complexity of the process in order to explain and demonstrate at a level appropriate to the children's needs. Many opportunities to use dictionaries need to be provided so that learners have plenty of practice. The investigations proposed by the new NLS Spelling Bank (2000) materials offer many possibilities.

In order to be able to use dictionaries to check and improve spellings, children need to have knowledge of how particular phonemes might be represented in writing so they need good basic knowledge of initial sounds, blends and digraphs. If they do not have this there is little point in trying to locate a particular word. Once you feel the learner is ready to make use of this basic knowledge, you should demonstrate, either as a class lesson or to individuals, how to go about looking up a word.

• Give young children as much experience as possible of working with the letters of the alphabet so that alphabetical order becomes familiar:
  – making themed alphabets;
  – read aloud and let children read alphabet books;
  – sorting books on shelves into alphabetical order by author;
  – ask children, in pairs, to write the letter which comes before or after a letter given by you (small individual whiteboards are useful for this);
  – using individual dictionaries, play games in which children have to see how quickly they can find the section for the letter (or word) given by you. This gives practice in becoming familiar with the quartiles and the letters in them.

• Give children lists of words, initially beginning with different letters, moving on to words beginning with the same letter, to sequence into alphabetical order.

• Once they can do this, give words for them to sequence and then find their meanings. Definitions can be written on prepared sheets – this could be a good group activity for literacy hour work.

• Show children how to set about finding a word which they are unsure how to spell. Ask them to suggest what the initial letter might be and then go on to consider the next phoneme(s) and how they might be written. Try all suggestions until the correct one is found. Finding a word which the child is unsure how to spell can be difficult for the beginner speller and children need practice and encouragement.

• Provide children with a sheet on which two headwords are written. With this give a list of words, some of which come between those headwords and some of which do not. Ask the children to put the words which belong on that page into alphabetical order and to discard those which do not.

• For work looking at the history, origins and roots of English words, make sure that etymological dictionaries are available so that children can seek information about the words. Provide keys to the abbreviations used (see Chapter 4).

• Make sure the classroom for older children is resourced with different kinds of dictionaries, ranging from simple alphabetic word lists (often Picture Dictionaries) to adult dictionaries from different publishers. Encourage children to compare definitions of words.

The thesaurus

Subject facts

The thesaurus complements the dictionary. The dictionary enables us to find the meaning of a word whilst the thesaurus helps to locate a word when we have only the meaning in mind.

Roget's Thesaurus divides words into six broad classifications which are subdivided to make location of the words in the field of search easier. There is also an alphabetical index to aid location of words.

However, Roget's Thesaurus is really only suitable for adult use. Most children's thesauruses use much simplified versions of this organisation and consist of lists of words which are synonyms or are related in some way, organised alphabetically.

How to use a thesaurus

The need for a thesaurus usually arises when children are found to be repeating the same vocabulary in their writing. A teacher may wish to intervene during the stage when writing is being redrafted, to suggest that alternative words could often be found which will minimise repetition. Children will need to be taught how to use a thesaurus and how to read the entries, though if they are used to using dictionaries, this will not prove difficult because of the alphabetical organisation and familiar abbreviations.

Look for alternatives to the word silly in Chambers Thesaurus (1991)
silly *adj.* absurd, addled, asinine, benumbed, bird-brained, brainless, childish, cuckoo, daft, dazed, dopey, drippy, fatuous, feather-brained, flighty, foolhardy, foolish, frivolous, gaga, giddy, groggy, hen-witted, idiotic, illogical, immature, imprudent, inane, inappropriate, inept, irrational, irresponsible, meaningless, mindless, muzzy, pointless, preposterous, puerile, ridiculous, scatter-brained, senseless, spoony, stunned, stupefied, stupid, unwise, witless.
N. clot, dope, duffer, goose, half-wit, ignoramus, ninny, silly-billy, simpleton, twit, wally.
Antonyms – collected, mature, sane, sensible, wise.

Most children will be able to find an alternative here! The only problem is that the meanings of the words are not given and many are slang or colloquial vocabulary. Teachers will need to discuss the appropriateness of alternatives with children and children will often need to turn to a dictionary in order to check the meaning of unfamiliar words.

Resources

References and further reading

Collins English Dictionary (5th edition, 2000), Glasgow: Harper Collins

Concise Oxford Dictionary (1982 edition), Oxford: Oxford University Press

Cripps, C and Cox, R (1990) *Joining the ABC,* Wisbech, Cambs: LDA

Deary, T (1996) *Wicked Words (Horrible Histories)*, Scholastic

Dutch, RA (ed) *Roget's Thesaurus* (1983), Harmondsworth: Penguin Books Ltd

Gentry, R (1982) 'An analysis of Developmental Spelling in GNYS AT WRK' in *The Reading Teacher* Vol. 36 (2)

Ferriero and Teberosky (1979) *Literacy Before Schooling,* USA: Heinemann

Hawker, GT (ed) (1992) *Spell it Yourself,* Oxford: Oxford University Press

Jarman, C (1982) *Jarman Handwriting Scheme*, Hemel Hempsted: Simon and Schuster

Johnson, Dr Samuel (1755) *A Dictionary of the English Language*

National Curriculum Handbook for Primary Teachers in England Key Stages 1 & 2 (1999), London: DfEE/QCA

National Literacy Strategy (1999) *Progression in Phonics,* London: DfEE

National Literacy Strategy (2000) *Spelling Bank,* London: DfEE

O'Sullivan, O and Thomas, A (2000) *Understanding Spelling,* London: CLPE

Palmer, Sue (1998) *A Simple Rhyming Dictionary,* (Pelican Big Book), London: Longman

Palmer, Sue (1998) *Words Borrowed from Other Languages* (Pelican Big Book), London: Longman

Peters, M (1985) *Spelling: Caught or Taught?,* London: Routledge and Kegan Paul

Sassoon, R (1990) *Handwriting: A New Perspective*, London: Stanley Thornes

Sassoon, R (1999) *Handwriting of the Twentieth Century*, London: Routledge/Falmer

Sassoon, R (1990) *Handwriting: the way to teach it*, London: Stanley Thornes

Torbe, M (1995) *Teaching and Learning Spelling*, East Grinstead: Ward Lock Educational

Dictionaries

Allen, RE (ed) (1990) *The Oxford Spelling Dictionary*, Oxford: Oxford University Press

HarperCollins publish a range of dictionaries for different ages:

> *Collins Early Dictionary*
> *Collins Emergent Dictionary*
> *Collins New School Dictionary*

Oxford University Press publish a range of dictionaries for different ages:

> *My Very First Oxford Dictionary* (available in big book edition)
> *The Oxford Primary School Dictionary*
> *The Oxford Primary School Thesaurus*

Dorling Kindersley

> *Dorling Kindersley Children's Illustrated Dictionary*
> *Dorling Kindersley First Dictionary*

ICT resources

Oxford Compendium on CD for WINPC (includes *Concise Oxford Dictionary* and *Oxford Thesaurus*) Oxford University Press e-mail: ep.info@oup.co.uk

Dorling Kindersley Children's Dictionary CD-ROM (WIN)

Dorling Kindersley *My First Incredible Amazing Dictionary* CD-ROM (Win/Mac)

Fisher-Price A-B-Cs ABLAC on CD for WINPC ABLAC Learning Words, Newton Abbot e-mail: educ@ablac.co.uk

Don Johnston for Mac, *Co-Writer* (Spellcheck package which offers possible words once a few letters have been typed in)

Don Johnston Special Needs homepage: http://donjonston.com

Chapter 3
Word structure and spelling conventions

This chapter looks at the ways in which words in English are constructed. Investigation of the underlying principles reveals the consistency and orderliness of the English *lexicon* (the vocabulary of the language) and understanding of these principles makes spelling words much more straightforward. The starting point for consideration of words is *morphology*.

English spelling has a large range of consistent, recognisable patterns and conventions. Hard and fast rules are fewer but where these are reliable they are explained here. It is better for learners to start by looking at patterns and then generalising rather than being given prescriptive rules first.

This chapter considers spellings related to the grammar of the language, at word families and at compound words. It also looks at abbreviations, homonyms, synonyms and antonyms.

Morphology

Subject facts

English spelling reflects very strongly the units of *meaning* in words. A *morpheme* is the smallest unit of meaning in a word. Crystal (1995) defines morphemes as 'the elements out of which words can be constructed' or (1987) 'the smallest meaningful elements into which words can be analysed'.

Morphology is the study of the structure of words. Our understanding of this structure and of how morphemes work can be of great help in spelling.

Many words in English cannot be divided into smaller units of meaning – they exist only as a *base* form. This is usually called the *root* (the term *stem* is sometimes used). In words like *house, school, no, castle,* there is one unit of meaning *(morpheme)*; the words cannot be divided into separate units of meaning.

Other words, however, are made up of more than one unit of meaning. For example:

disappear – dis + appear. The *root* word is *appear* and another unit of meaning *(morpheme)* has been added before the root – this is a *prefix (dis)*. The addition of this unit of meaning creates a new word with the opposite meaning. Similarly:

useful – use + ful. The *root* word is *use* and another unit of meaning has been added after the root – this is a *suffix (ful)*. The addition of this new unit of meaning creates a new word, turning the noun, *use,* into an adjective: *useful.*

Units of meaning in English can be added both before and after the root; these added units of meaning are called *affixes.* Affixes which precede the root word are called *prefixes.* Affixes which follow the root word are called *suffixes.* Both the affixes and the roots to which they are attached are called *morphemes.* It is possible to attach more than one additional unit of meaning (morphemes) to one root: *disappearance – dis + appear + ance.*

The prefix *dis-* adds a negative meaning to *appear;* the suffix *-ance* changes the verb *appear* to the noun *appearance.* In other words, the root word *appear,* which was a verb, becomes a noun *appearance;* this positive noun is changed to negative, by the addition of *dis-.*

All affixes (prefixes and suffixes) are morphemes.

Types of morpheme

Free morphemes stand alone as a unit of meaning, for example, *house, school, dog, talk.*

It is possible to combine two free morphemes (for example, two words) to make a new (compound) word, for example, *houseboat / house + boat; housewife / house + wife; schoolboy / school + boy.*

Bound morphemes cannot stand alone but must be attached (bound) to other morphemes in order to reveal their meaning, for example, *house (s), school (s), dog (s).*

In each case the *s* is a bound morpheme, changing the meaning from singular to plural. The *s* shows that there is more than one house, school, dog – that is, it *adds* meaning to the root word.

Any of the following four bound morphemes can be added to the root *(talk)*, to add meaning.

Talk (s) (ing) (ed) (er)

talk (free morpheme)	verb or noun
talk + s (bound morpheme)	present tense of the verb or plural noun
talk + ing (bound morpheme)	present participle of the verb
talk + ed (bound morpheme)	past tense/past participle of the verb

These bound morphemes are all *inflectional suffixes* – that is, they mark *grammatical differences*.

talk + er (bound morpheme)	a new noun (one who talks)

The addition of the bound morpheme *er* creates a new word and is thus a *derivational suffix*.

Suffixes and prefixes

Inflectional suffixes

In English, there are few inflectional suffixes; all are *bound morphemes*. They attach to *nouns* (to show plurals or possession), to *verbs* (to show the tense or the person) and to *adjectives* (to show comparative and superlative).

The following list includes all inflectional suffixes in English:

Role of suffix	Suffix(es)	Examples
noun plural	-s, -es, -ies	cup**s**, box**es**, fl**ies**
genitive case (possession)	-'s, -s'	the boy**'s** book
		the two boy**s'** books
3rd person singular	-es, -s	he like**s** the book
(present tense)		she wish**es** to leave
(past tense)	**-ed**	he walk**ed** slowly
contracted negative	**-n't**	is**n't**, were**n't**
-ing (present participle) form	**-ing**	go**ing**, say**ing**
-ed/-en (past participle) form	**ed**	I have finish**ed**
		the game was finish**ed**
		I have eat**en**
-er comparison	**-er**	bigg**er**, happi**er**
-est superlative	**-est**	bigg**est**, happi**est**

Derivational suffixes

There are many derivational suffixes in English; they are also *bound morphemes*. Their purpose is to change the meaning of the base form of the word to create a new word. Adding a derivational suffix to the base word (root) often changes the class of the word. These include:

Word structure and spelling conventions

Role of suffix	Examples
abstract noun makers	mile (n.) + **-age** (suffix) / mileage (abstract noun)
	slave (n.) + **-ery** (suffix) / slavery (abstract noun)
	friend (n.) + **-ship** (suffix) / friendship (abstract noun)
concrete noun makers	book (n.) + **-let** (suffix) / booklet (concrete noun)
	cook (v.) or (n.) + **-er** (suffix) / cooker (concrete noun)
adverb makers	happy (adj.) + **-ly** (suffix) / happily (adv.)
	nice (adj.) + **-ly** (suffix) / nicely (adv.)
verb makers	deaf (adj.) + **-en** (suffix) / deafen (v.)
	beauty (n.) + **-fy** (suffix) / beautify (v.)
nouns from verbs	build (v.) + **-ing** (suffix) / building (n.)
	write (v.) + **-er** (suffix) / writer (n.)
	refuse (v.) + **-al** (suffix) / refusal (n.)
nouns from adjectives	happy (adj.) + **-ness** (suffix) / happiness (n.)
adjectives from nouns	hair (n.) + **-y** (suffix) / hairy (adj.)
	success (n.) + **-ful** (suffix) / successful (adj.)
	care (n.) + **-less** (suffix) / careless (adj.)
adjectives from verbs	drink (v.) + **-able** (suffix) / drinkable

Prefixes (added before the base word or *root*) are entirely *derivational* – that is, they form new words or new meanings. There are not a great number of these and their meanings are consistent. Many of these prefixes add a negative meaning to the base word and will be immediately recognisable.

> **dis** + **appear** (the opposite of appear)
> **mis** + **behave** (the opposite of behave)
> **in** + **attentive** (the opposite of attentive)
> **im** + **possible** (the opposite of possible)
> **un** + **happy** (the opposite of happy)

The addition of the negative prefix does not change the class of these words.

> **appear** and **disappear** are both verbs
> **behave** and **misbehave** are both verbs
> **attentive** and **inattentive** are both adjectives
> **possible** and **impossible** are both adjectives
> **happy** and **unhappy** are both adjectives

It is sometimes difficult to give a precise definition of the meaning of some common prefixes, though the words they create are not difficult to understand.

en-/em-	**en**danger, **en**able, **en**close, **em**power, **em**battle, **em**bankment (where the meaning is to do with bringing about)
re-	**re**arrange, **re**appear, **re**petition, **re**turn, **re**place, **re**new, **re**tell (where the meaning is usually *again* or *back*)
be-	**be**grudge, **be**set, **be**moan, **be**friend, **be**spectacled, **be**little (where the meaning is to do with surrounding or making)

In many cases these do change the class of the word, often creating verbs.

Other common prefixes in English include those which are derived from Latin or Greek words. When these prefixes are used, the meaning of the prefix is always consistent.

anti-	(against) as in **anti**clockwise, **anti**biotic
ante-	(before) as in **ante**natal, **ante**chamber
ex-	(out of) as in **ex**port, **ex**clude
inter-	(between) as in **inter**national, **inter**sect
post-	(after) as in **post**pone, **post**script
pre-	(before) as in **pre**fix, **pre**historic
sub-	(under) as in **sub**marine, **sub**conscious, **sub**text
super-	(above) as in **super**visor, **super**natural, **super**man
trans-	(across) as in **trans**atlantic, **trans**cribe
under-	(below/beneath) as in **under**study, **under**ground, **under**graduate

See pages 118 and 130 for more information on Latin and Greek influences on English.

Affixes – conventions and rules

An affix can be either a prefix (added before the root) or a suffix (added after the root). There are a number of consistent rules relating to the addition of affixes to base words.

Prefixes

With the negative prefixes *dis-*, *de-*, *mis-*, *un-*, *in-/im-/ir-/il-* the following rules apply:

1. The straightforward rule is that the prefix is added to the base word. So, if the first letter of the base word is the same as the last letter of the prefix, this will result in that letter being doubled where the two morphemes join.

de- + fuse /	defuse
mis- + behave /	misbehave
un- + happy /	unhappy
un- + necessary /	un**nn**ecessary
dis- + honest /	dishonest
dis- + satisfied /	dis**ss**atisfied

2. The *in-* prefix can become *im-*, *ir-*, *il-*, usually because the change makes pronunciation smoother.

in- + visible /	invisible
in- + correct /	incorrect
in- + numerate /	in**nn**umerate

Before the letters *p* or *m* or *b* at the start of the base word, *in-* becomes *im-*.

im- + possible /	impossible
im- + patient /	impatient
im- + mortal /	im**mm**ortal
im- + moral /	im**mm**oral
im- + balance /	imbalance

Before a letter *l* at the start of the base word, *in-* becomes *il-*.

il- + literate /	**il**literate
il- + legible /	**il**legible

Before a letter *r* at the start of the base word, *in-* becomes *ir-*.

ir- + regular /	**ir**regular
ir- + responsible /	**ir**responsible

Note that the rule about adding with no omissions still results in the double consonant in the middle.

The same rule applies for other (non-negative) prefixes, though words are sometimes hyphenated.

pre- + scribe /	prescribe	
pre- + record /	pre-record	
sub- + merge /	submerge	
sub- + zero /	sub-zero	
non- + sense /	nonsense	The prefix **non-** is most
non- + stop /	non-stop	often hyphenated to the
non- + fiction /	non-fiction	root word
co- + incidence /	coincidence	
co- + operate /	co-operate	
re- + make /	remake	
re- + count /	recount	
re- + read /	reread	

Note that when **re-** is followed by a root word beginning with *e*, the two parts are hyphenated.

re- + entry /	re-entry
re- + examine /	re-examine

A note on hyphenation
The hyphen is often used where the prefix ends with the same letter that the root word begins with *(co-operate, re-entry)*, or to clarify pronunciation *(pre-record, pre-empt)*. It is also used to distinguish differences in meaning:

re- + count can be **re**count (narrate/tell) or **re**-count (count again)
re- + cover can be **re**cover (get back) or **re**-cover (to cover again)
re- + form can be **re**form (make better) or **re**-form (form again)

See also page 90 on compound words.

Suffixes

Suffixes, whether inflectional or derivational, can begin with either a consonant or a vowel. The NLS differentiates suffixes according to whether they are *vowel suffixes* or *consonant suffixes*. The inflectional/derivational distinction is, however, important for teachers if we are to understand the roles of the two kinds of suffix in modifying root words.

Presenting to children a set of rules, such as those that follow, is not helpful as a starting point for work on suffixes. Activities which encourage children to look closely at words and add or take off suffixes can help them to see how the system works. They can then see the generalisation or rule in operation and will understand how it works.

Consonant suffixes (-ful, -ness, -ly, -ment, -less)

These are generally added to the base word without modification, except when the word ends with a consonant + *y*, when the *y* is changed to *i*.

Base word		Suffix	New word
care	+	**-less**	careless
care	+	**-ful**	careful
pain	+	**-less**	painless
pain	+	**-ful**	painful
friend	+	**-ly**	friendly
friend	+	**-less**	friendless
like	+	**-ness**	likeness
like	+	**-ly**	likely
ship	+	**-ment**	shipment
beauty	+	**-ful**	beautiful
pity	+	**-ful**	pitiful
pity	+	**-less**	pitiless
joy	+	**-ful**	joyful
joy	+	**-less**	joyless
employ	+	**-ment**	employment

In these last two words the **y** is preceded by a vowel and the two letters together make a vowel digraph, so the **y** does not change to **i**.

There are exceptions relating to the addition of consonant suffixes to words ending in *e*, for example, true – truly; argue – argument. These should be pointed out to children.

Vowel suffixes
The conventions about adding vowel suffixes are more complex in relation to the base words and the vowels they contain. The vowel suffixes include all the inflectional suffixes (which indicate tense, plurals, comparison – see above).

1. If the base word ends in *e* then it must be dropped before the suffix is added. If the base word ends with a consonant followed by *y*, the *y* changes to *i*, except when adding *-ing*.

Base word		Suffix	New word
drive	+	**-er**	driver
drive	+	**-ing**	driving
drive	+	**-able**	drivable
farm	+	**-ing**	farming
farm	+	**-ed**	farmed
farm	+	**-er**	farmer
believe	+	**-ing**	believing
believe	+	**-ed**	believed
believe	+	**-er**	believer
believe	+	**-able**	believable
play	+	**-ing**	playing
play	+	**-ed**	played
play	+	**-er**	player
play	+	**-able**	playable
carry	+	**-ed**	(**-y**+ **-i**) carried
carry	+	**-er**	(**-y** + **-i**) carrier
carry	+	**-ing**	carrying

The exceptions of *-able* and *-ous* added to words ending with *-ce* or *-ge* should be pointed out to children, for example, *notice + able = noticeable; courage + ous = courageous.* The retention of the *e* ensures the *c* and the *g* keep the soft *c* and *g* sound.

2. When vowel suffixes are added to words (often one-syllable words) with a short vowel sound, the final consonant is doubled when the suffix is added, to mark the retention of the short vowel sound and/or the stressed syllable.

Base word		Suffix	New word
shop	+	**-ing**	shopping
shop	+	**-ed**	shopped
shop	+	**-er**	shopper
bat	+	**-ing**	batting
bat	+	**-ed**	batted
forget	+	**-ing**	forgetting
forget	+	**-en (note change of e to o)**	forgotten
forget	+	**-able**	forgettable
begin	+	**-er**	beginner
begin	+	**-ing**	beginning
commit	+	**-ed**	committed
commit	+	**-ing**	committing
commit	+	**-al**	committal
commit	+	**-ee**	committee
refer	+	**-ed**	referred
refer	+	**-ing**	referring
refer	+	**-al**	referral

Note that this final example (like **prefer** and **transfer**) does not consistently follow the rule:

refer	+	ence	reference
refer	+	ee	referee

In these two words the stress does not fall on the final syllable of the base word (**refer**) but on the first syllable (**reference**) or the suffix (**referee**).

An understanding of the structure of words helps spellers to see the consistency and logic of word meanings. The role of the different kinds of suffixes and prefixes, and the consistency with which rules relating to them are applied should be demonstrated, especially to older children. Though teachers would not necessarily use the inflectional/ derivational terminology, it is important that they understand the distinction. Affixes (prefixes and suffixes) can be a profitable field of investigation for children, enabling them to generalise and see the patterns. Knowledge of the way in which affixes work and the rules which govern the way they are added to base words can be of assistance in spelling. The NLS materials for Key Stage 2 Spelling (2000) contain many activities for children which focus on these. To be able to explain clearly and to guide children's investigations, teachers need to be familiar with the generalisations and rules. Although there are exceptions, there is sufficient consistency in the ways affixes are added for the rules to be useful, although they should be demonstrated through work with many examples so that learners can see the rules in operation.

There is often confusion over whether the final consonant doubles in two-syllable words ending in *t*. Whilst single syllable words generally do double the consonant when vowel suffixes are added (fit – fitter – fitting; get – getting), two-syllable words, which look the same, do not:

Common misconceptions

Base word		Suffix	New word
benefit	+	**-ing**	benefiting
benefit	+	**-ed**	benefited
target	+	**-ing**	targeting
target	+	**-ed**	targeted
target	+	**-able**	targetable

This confusion is the reason for the frequent misspelling of these two words.

The reason for the differences in spelling lies in the stress on the syllables in the words. The monosyllabic words *fit* and *get* just like *sit, hit, spit,* have a single stress on the one syllable. In *benefit, target, limit,* and so on, the stress is on the first syllable, not the one to which the suffix is to be added, so the final consonant of this syllable does not double.

The generalisation about doubling and the stressed syllables does not, however, apply for most vowel suffixes with base words ending in *l*.

Base word		Suffix	New word
travel	+	**-er**	traveller
travel	+	**-ing**	travelling
travel	+	**-ed**	travelled
libel	+	**-ed**	libelled
libel	+	**-ing**	libelling
libel	+	**-er**	libeller
libel	+	**-ous**	libellous

Although the stress in these words is on the first syllable, the *l* is doubled when the vowel suffix is added.

There are, inevitably, exceptions! When the vowel suffixes *-ise*, and *-ity* are added, the single *l* remains:

Base word		Suffix	New word
equal	+	**-ise**	equalise
equal	+	**-ity**	equality
local	+	**-ise**	localise
local	+	**-ity**	locality

The rule about doubling the final consonant of the base word is still a matter of debate in the case of *focus*.

Base word		Suffix	New word
focus	+	**-ing**	focusing
focus	+	**-ing**	focussing

Either form is accepted as correct at the present time, though individuals often have a strong preference for one or the other. It is possible that before long, usage in published texts will influence users of the word to opt for the single *s* form.

Teaching ideas

Word level work for the National Literacy Strategy includes work on prefixes (*un-* and *dis-*) and suffixes (*-ful* and *-ly*) as early as Year 2, though the terminology is not introduced until later. Much teaching can be done through games.

• Make cards with the prefixes *un-* and *dis-* and sets of words to which these can be added. Children use the cards to add a prefix to the base word and create new words, which they list on a prepared sheet:

Base word	New word	Meaning

When they are used to the game, include some words to which both prefixes can be added, for example, *like* (can add either, to create different meanings: 'His bag is unlike mine', 'I dislike the colour of his bag'); *cover* (can add either to create different meanings: 'She went to uncover the table', 'Can you discover where the treasure is hidden?')

- Similar games can be devised for other common prefixes *(in-, -mis-, ex-, de-, re-)*.

- Prepare card sets for common suffixes *(-ly, -ful, -ness)* and add to base words. Show how words ending in *y* change the *y* to *i* when the suffix is added. Ask the children whether there are any exceptions to this – the hunt for these will ensure children compile substantial lists of words! They will not find any.

- Use old newspapers/magazines and highlighter pens and ask children to highlight different prefixes or suffixes in a separate colour. The use of old newspapers has the advantage of providing an inexhaustible supply of print for similar activities.

- Make lists of verbs and add inflectional suffix *-ed*. Classify these to show where:
   i) *-ed* is simply added (as in *talk – talked*)
   ii) adding *-ed* doubles the consonant (as in *drop – dropped*)
   iii) verbs ending in *e* add only *d* (as in *save – saved*)
   iv) verbs ending in *y* change the *y* to *i* to add *-ed* (as in *try – tried*).
Ask the children to work out the rules for adding *–ed*.

- Do a similar activity adding *-ing* to the verb. They should notice the *y* to *i* rule is different *(try – tried – trying)*.

- Make collections of words with the same suffix, especially the more unusual ones *(-al, -ism, -ic, -ise, -ship, -hood)*, and display these.

- Make collections of groups of words created by the addition of suffixes to base words and display these, for example, *care: care–ful, care–ful–ly, care–ful–ness, care–less, care–less-ness, car–ing, car–ed, car–er, car–ing–ly*. Point out how many have two suffixes added.
   To develop this, select words to which multiple suffixes can be added. Ask children to investigate how many can be added, for example, *thank: thank–ful, thank–ful–ly, thank–ful–ness, thank–less, thank–less-ness*. Make sure some words are included which use less common suffixes, for example, *correct: correc(t)–ion, correct–ive, correct–able, correct–ly*.

Word families

Subject facts

It is very important to understanding how a base word, with the addition of affixes, can create a collection of words with consistent spelling patterns, especially when the spelling of a related word does not sound the same. The range of words which can be made is known as the *derivational field*. It is also important for children to see that meanings of words in the family are related.

Exploration of word families can be a helpful way of seeing generalisations or rules about adding different affixes:

sign	signed	signing	signature
	significant	signify	significance
	insignificant	signpost	signatory
	design	resign	signal
finite	finish	finished	finishing
	final	finalise	infinite
	infinity	define	definite
	definition		

Other base words which can usefully be explored include: *care, different, front, help, manage, medicine, music, part, play, script, use.*

The number of possible word families is vast!

Adjectives: comparative and superlative

This is a particular aspect of looking at word families about which children can generalise. The comparison of adjectives is achieved by means of the *inflectional suffixes -er* and *-est*.

The base form of the adjective is the *absolute form*. The addition of the inflections increase the degree of quality of the adjective in two steps – the *comparative* form and the *superlative* form:

Absolute form	Comparative	Superlative
big	bigger	biggest
happy	happier	happiest
long	longer	longest
quiet	quieter	quietest

The meaning of the *-er* inflection is *more* and the meaning of the *-est* inflection is *most*. There are some adjectives where the inflectional suffixes which show increase in degree cannot be used. These are mostly three or more syllable adjectives, for example, *beautiful, interesting.* These adjectives are compared using the words *more* and *most*.

Absolute form	Comparative	Superlative
beautiful	more beautiful	most beautiful
comfortable	more comfortable	most comfortable
careless	more careless	most careless

Many young children will use the regular form incorrectly to start with in some words: they will say 'beautifuller' or 'favouritest'. But, like other errors where children overgeneralise a rule, this is usually developmental and ceases once a child is familiar with the irregular forms.

Some two-syllable adjectives can use either way of comparing and the choice really depends on the style or the sound of the sentence.

Absolute form	Comparative	Superlative
common	commoner	commonest
common	more common	most common

There are few irregular comparatives. The most common of these are:

Absolute form	Comparative	Superlative
good	better	best
bad	worse	worst
little	less	least

Understanding how words are built up from their constituent parts, how the morphemes fit together in a consistent way, makes spelling even long words much more manageable. Once those units of meaning can be seen to be consistent and logical, the complexity of very many words is reduced. Children need to have the underlying principles explained to them, so teachers must have the knowledge to do this.

Why you need to know these facts

The adjective *old* has regular comparative and superlative forms: *old – older – oldest*. For example, *This is an old book; this one is older, but this first edition is the oldest.*

There is also an irregular form, used when referring to family members: *old – elder – eldest*. It is considered correct to say *elder* when comparing two people. For example, *Peter and James are brothers. Peter is the elder* (of the two). However, *Ellen, Jane and Maggie are sisters. Ellen is the eldest* (of the three).

This makes sense if the meanings of 'more old' *(elder)* and 'most old' *(eldest)* are considered.

The regular form, *(old, older, oldest)*, is often incorrectly used; people will sometimes say *'I am the oldest in my family.'*

This variation in what is currently considered correct usage will probably change over time, so that the regular comparative and superlative forms of *old* will become accepted in all circumstances.

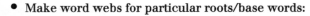

Teaching ideas

- Make word webs for particular roots/base words:

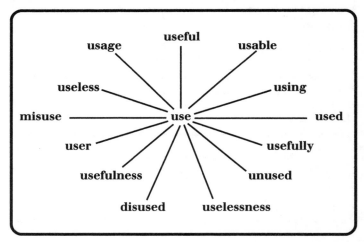

The word webs can be collected in children's spelling books and used for reference. The most common ones can be displayed for class reference.

- Look at suffix families. Make a collection of words with the same suffix and look at what kinds of words (nouns, adjectives, and so on) these make. For example, *-cian*:

musician, optician, physician, magician, electrician, politician; -ic: terrific, comic, energetic, scientific, photographic, electronic. Investigate whether these suffixes ever produce words of a different class.

● Aspects of word-family work can link with work on grammar (word classes). Provide the children with a list of nouns and ask them to find a verb in the same family.

Nouns	Verbs
speech	speak
flight	fly
gift	give
life	live
knowledge	know
advert	advertise

This could be done the other way round, or with other parts of speech.

Noun	Adjective
education	educational
comedy	comic
courage	courageous
beauty	beautiful

● Give children examples of absolute forms of adjectives. Ask them to sort these into two sets – those which add *-er* and *-est* for the comparative and superlative and those which use the *more/most* form. What do they notice about the adjectives in each category?

Inflectional suffixes – plurals and possession

Subject facts

Plural suffixes (-s, –es, –ies)

Most nouns in English have both a *singular* and a *plural* form, expressing the difference between one (singular) and more than one (plural).

The vast majority of nouns in English simply add the inflectional suffix *s* to show the plural. This includes those which end with a silent *e* such as *gate* or *mile*.

Singular	Plural
book	books
comb	combs
nest	nests
bank	banks
farm	farms
bath	baths
nail	nails
clock	clocks
number	numbers
voice	voices
stone	stones

It will be clear from this list that a great range of consonants, consonant blends and digraphs all follow this regular form.

When nouns end in *o* they usually add *s* to make the plural.

Singular	Plural
radio	radios
zoo	zoos
solo	solos

but there are some well-known exceptions, which add *-es*.

Exceptions	
potato	potato**es**
volcano	volcano**es**
hero	hero**es**

When the noun ends with a *sibilant* (an /s/-like sound) and there is no silent *e*, the plural is formed by adding *-es*.

Singular	Plural
bus	buses
glass	glasses
church	churches
wish	wishes
fox	foxes
buzz	buzzes

When the noun ends with *y* preceded by a consonant, the *y* is replaced by *i* and *-es*.

Singular	Plural
fly	flies
daisy	daisies
puppy	puppies
enemy	enemies

If the *y* is preceded by a vowel, the *y* remains unchanged.

Singular	Plural
boy	boys
holiday	holidays
donkey	donkeys

There are groups of nouns which have exceptional plural forms. All of these have their roots in Old English or Germanic language influences.

1. Some with a final sound *f*, change *f* to *v* before adding *-es* to make the plural.

Singular	Plural
knife	knives
life	lives
half	halves
leaf	leaves
self (myself)	selves (ourselves)
Some nouns do not make this change:	
roof	roofs

In the case of the following four nouns, either form is acceptable, though modern usage seems to favour making no change.

Singular	Plural
dwarf	dwarfs/dwarves
scarf	scarfs/scarves
hoof	hoofs/hooves
wharf	wharfs/wharves

2. Seven nouns change their vowel in the plural.

Singular	Plural
man	men
woman	women
foot	feet
tooth	teeth
goose	geese
mouse	mice
louse	lice

3. A few nouns remain the same in both the singular and the plural.

Singular	Plural
sheep	sheep
deer	deer
aircraft	aircraft
species	species

The names of many fish do not change between the singular and the plural.

Singular	Plural
salmon	salmon
trout	trout
cod	cod

But some do:

Singular	Plural
crab	crabs
herring	herrings
shark	sharks

Some generic terms can be used in either form in the plural, depending on the context.

Singular	Plural
fish	fish/fishes
meat	meat/meats
fruit	fruit/fruits

4. The Old English *n* plural marker survives in very few words.

Singular	Plural
child	children
ox	oxen
brother	brethren

Possession

Possession is shown by the inflection *-'s* or *-s'*. It is important to distinguish between the use of the *apostrophe* in *contractions*, for example, *didn't, I've,* and the apostrophe used to show *possession* (belonging to/of).

The apostrophe is used with nouns, but not with pronouns. There is a set of possessive pronouns which express ownership or 'belonging' – some of which do not have an *s* at the end and therefore cause little confusion. Those ending in *s* do often cause confusion.

Possessive pronouns

Used with a noun	Used alone
my	mine
your	yours
his, her, its	his, hers
our	ours
their	theirs
whose	

The most common mistake is to put an apostrophe in *its* (*it's*) because it is assumed to be like the possessive form for nouns (*girl's*) (see below). *Its* is a pronoun. Mistakes are made, also, with several of the *s* endings. Older children would benefit from looking at the whole set of possessive pronouns so that they can see the way they work.

In order to express possession in relation to nouns, there are two forms. There is no detectable difference between the two in speech, but they are represented differently in writing. The *singular* form uses an apostrophe *before an added s*, for example, *the boy's book, the man's hat, the summer's day, Santa's workshop.*

When the noun is plural, the *s* is already present, so, rather than write two *ss*, the apostrophe is placed *after the final s*, for example, *Here are the girls' coats, There are the two boys' books, The ladies' hairdresser.*

When the plural noun has an irregular plural form which does not end with *s*, the -*s* is added as it is for singular nouns, for example, *The children's teacher, The men's cars, The women's watches.*

Why you need to know these facts

The possessive apostrophe is so commonly misapplied that children are surrounded by environmental print where it is written incorrectly or added when it is not needed.

Children should have the form explained to them so that they understand that it is different from the contraction apostrophe which indicates that something has been missed out. The possessive apostrophe does not show that there are letters missing, but has a quite different purpose and meaning. Children can be taught a simple check to see whether an apostrophe is needed (see below).

Common misconceptions

The apostrophe is commonly misplaced with decade dates. There is neither possession nor contraction involved in these forms:

> Secondary education was reorganised in the 1960s and 1970s.
> My grandmother grew up in the 1940s.

An apostrophe is often incorrectly inserted (*1970's*). As the meaning of 1970s is simply plural, no apostrophe is required. An apostrophe sometimes needs to be added after the *s*, when the meaning is *of the/belonging to*:

> I like 60s' music. (Meaning I like the music belonging to the 60s.)
> I think 30s' furniture has become very expensive. (Meaning the furniture of the 30s.)

However, if the decade is abbreviated (40s, 60s, 70s) an apostrophe should be inserted before the numbers because the 19 has been omitted (1940s – '40s, 1960s – '60s, 1970s – '70s) (see page 99 for more on contractions).

Teaching ideas

• Make a collection of nouns related to a particular topic (perhaps a topic currently being studied, for example, Houses and Homes, Food, Games and Toys, Minibeasts, The Body). Write these on cards and make another set of cards with -s and -es plural endings on them. Ask children to use the cards to make the nouns into plurals and to list the plural forms. Use these to investigate generalisations about which words add -s and which add -es and then formulate these rules.

• When these forms are familiar, move on to words ending in y. Teach the rule about which words change y to ies and which simply add s. Make sets of words which are a mixture of those with y preceded by a vowel and those with y preceded by a consonant. Make sets of s endings and ies endings on small cards. In pairs, ask the children to fit the two parts together and then, when they have been checked, transfer the lists to their spelling books, together with the rule.

• Teach children these two ways of checking whether a possessive apostrophe is needed.

1. Demonstrate with simple sentences and explain the meaning:

> This is the girl's bicycle. (means) This is the bicycle belonging to the girl.
>
> He has his mother's book. (means) He has the book belonging to his mother.

If the sentence can be turned round using *the... belonging to* phrase, there should be an apostrophe *s*.

2. **Another way of checking is to put in** *his, her, their* **or** *its* **and see whether it makes sense.**

> 'My mother's book' – could you say 'my mother, (her) book' and keep the sense/ Yes – so 'mother's' needs the apostrophe.
> 'The school's motto' – could you say 'the school, (its) motto' and keep the sense/ Yes – so 'school's' needs the apostrophe.

Then give them some examples to try out the checks.

Homonyms, homographs and homophones

Subject facts

These terms are ones which are frequently confused and the definitions overlap. The NLS Glossary gives the following definitions:

> *homonym:* a word with the same spelling or pronunciation as another, but with a different meaning or origin. May be a *homograph* or *homophone*.
> *homograph:* a word with the same spelling as another, but different meaning. Pronunciation may be different.
> *homophone:* words which sound the same but have different meaning or different spelling.

From the above information it is clear that the generic term, *homonym*, is the one which may be least useful to children.

Concentrating on the two terms, *homograph* and *homophone*, which have clear links to the terms *grapheme* and *phoneme*, should be easier. If we remember that a grapheme is the written representation of a sound and a phoneme is the actual sound, the distinction becomes clearer.

Homographs
Some homographs are pronounced differently, even though the spelling is the same. The following examples demonstrate this.

lead	The pipes were made of lead.
lead	The dog was on a lead.
lead	The fastest runner took the lead.
lead	The homeless lead a miserable life.

Even when the pronunciation is the same, as in the above examples, the meanings are rather different.

Other homographs have the same spelling and are pronounced the same, but have different meanings.

calf	The calf had just been born.
calf	The footballer had a calf injury.
pole	They hung the curtains on a pole.
Pole	Jan's father was a Pole.

Homographs cause little problem in spelling (once the word is known) because the meaning is clear from the context of the sentence.

Homophones

For spelling, homophones present more problems because there are so many of them in English. Initially it is better not to teach homophones together because this can lead to even more confusion. It is important to focus on *meaning* rather than *sounds* in dealing with them and to link them with other related words.

> Teach *here* with the words related in meaning and having similar letter patterns: *there, where, somewhere, nowhere.* Teach *hear* with *ear, heard, hearing* (all related) or with *dear, fear, tear, weary, clear* and other words with the same letter pattern and a different sound: *bear, wear, learn, earn.*

Be aware, when you are teaching, that there are both homographs and homophones within the group!

> *tear* (to rip) and *tear* (liquid from the eye, though this is more commonly plural) – homographs
> *heard* (past tense of hear) and *herd* (of cattle) – homophones
> *bear* (large animal and to carry) and *bare* (naked) – homophones

Commonly confused homophones
It is helpful to concentrate on the meanings of all of these words.

There, their, they're
Teach *there* with the group above, but not with *their* or *they're*.
Teach *their* with the other possessive pronouns (see above) and *they're* with other contractions (see below).

To, two, too
to causes few problems but should be linked with other prepositions – *from, under, over, in, out , off, on.*
two should be taught with other numeral spellings (remember here *four*, to be separated from *for*).
too is the most difficult to teach but keeping the focus on meaning helps – remind children of *very* or *excessive* as one meaning and give lots of examples:

He was too late for school.
The room is too cold today.
I was too tired for work yesterday.
You finished that cake too quickly!

Show the other meaning of *as well* or *also* with examples, too!

John was late, too.
We are going on a trip, too.

Homophone jokes and puns
Homophones are a rich source of humour in children's jokes and using humour is an effective way through which homophones can be taught. Children love the humour of puns and, if encouraged, they will seek out jokes of this nature tirelessly.

Remember that the collection must be homophone jokes and that children should be able to explain the different meanings (and the different spellings) of the homophones.

Which tree is never alone/ A pear tree (because it is a pair).
What did the flour say to the water/ We'll be needed (kneaded) to make dough.
Why is a fog like a lost boy/ Because they are both missed (mist).

When teaching children about homophones we need to be able to talk about the structures of words to help them remember the differences. Considerable stress is placed on work with homophones in the NLS (2000) Key Stage 2 Spelling materials and there is work in both Year 4 and Year 5. They do seem to suggest teaching them together, but also add 'Analogy with family groups can be helpful.' Probably the most productive approach is through playing with words and capitalising on children's enjoyment of this.

• When children are older, devise 'Pairs' games in which homophones are written on cards. These are spread out face down, and players have to find matching pairs (either homophones or homographs). They can only claim a pair if they can give accurate definitions of the different meanings.

• The same cards can be used to play 'Snap'. Players can only keep the snapped cards if they can give the meanings of the pair which gave the snap.

• Make a class collection of all the homographs or homophones children can find. Whoever finds them is allowed to write them on a big poster.

• Make a class Joke Book of jokes which depend on homophones/homographs. Allow children to read these out at specified times, for example, the end of morning or afternoon, before home-time. The listeners can be asked to identify the two words involved in the joke.

• Have class homophone quizzes in teams. You provide a word and the child from one team must come to write a sentence (or two) which show the meanings, on the flip chart or whiteboard. For example, if given the words *bean* and *been*, the child might write *'I have just been writing about the beans growing.'*
    If a mistake is made and a member of the other team can correct it, the points for that homophone go to that team.

• Combine dictionary work with work on homophones. Write one of a pair (or trio) of homophones on the board. Children have individual dictionaries and have to find the other word(s) with the same sound. This could be a 'quick response' competition, with points awarded for the first child to identify correctly the homophone. Words can be graded in difficulty or similarity of spelling, according to the experience of the children. For example, words which have the same starting letters will be easier to find than those which are spelled very differently.

> Easier pairs: beach/beech, hair/hare, made/maid, week/weak, hear/here.
> Harder pairs: aloud/allowed, hire/higher, weather/whether, seen/scene, write/right, rap/wrap.

Compound words

Subject facts

Compound words are formed by putting together two existing words to convey a single new idea. Each part of the word is a *free morpheme*, that is each part can stand alone (see page 64). The two words which are brought together rarely change their spelling: they are spelled the same as when they are separate words:

classroom	sunshine
blackboard/whiteboard	football
birthday	hairbrush
blackbird	somebody
armchair	headache
suitcase	earthquake
typewritten	homesick
heartbroken	honeymoon
malthouse	snowman
toadstool	fortnight

Most of the words formed in this way are nouns.

The stress patterns in compound words are consistent. The first part of the word (the first morpheme) receives slightly greater stress than the second morpheme when the words are spoken.

Try saying the compound words in the list above and notice where the stress falls.

Exploration of the meanings of the two parts and how they have combined to create a new meaning often proves interesting.

Breakfast

The first meal of the day, is made up of *break + fast*. To *fast* is to go without food and this first meal interrupts or breaks that fast. So the meaning is very clear.

Windmill

This word is made up of *wind + mill*. A mill is used to grind grain to make flour – this was done between millstones which had to be turned. The power to turn the stones in the past was generated by the wind. Thus, the building in which the stones ground, and which was powered by the wind, came to be called a *windmill*.

There are many more compound words which can be investigated in this way. Some are very recent, such as *blackboard, whiteboard, keyboard, inkjet.* The investigations carried out will help children remember the spellings, as will generating 'new' compound words for modern objects and concepts.

A note on hyphenation

The use of a hyphen in compound words is often transitional. When new compounds are formed, they will often be hyphenated for some time, but usage will lead to the disappearance of the hyphen, for example, *flowerpot* is now the accepted form, but *flower-pot* is still seen; *whiteboard* is now accepted (because of the parallel with *blackboard*) but *white-board* is still seen. Whether hyphenated or not, such words are still known as compound words.

American English has far fewer hyphens in compound words than does British English, which tends to retain the separate words for longer.

Why you need to know these facts

Looking at compound words can help children understand the ways in which English is constantly evolving to incorporate new concepts and new artefacts. Until typewriters, hairbrushes or whiteboards existed, there was no need for these words. Much recent technological vocabulary (for example, *telecommunications, microbiology*) makes use of Greek and Latin root words, so work on compound words links well with work looking at these affixes.

Word structure and spelling conventions

- Provide copies of maps of the British Isles and look for placenames which are compound words, such as *Newcastle, Brownhill, Redbridge*. This will probably lead into further work on the meanings of the elements of placenames (see pages 110 and 115).

- Provide children with a set of base words and ask them to find as many compound words as they can which use these. They should then look at how the separate meanings have been combined to create a new meaning.

- Ask children to research the meanings of long-established compound words, such as *cupboard, sideboard, clockwise*. They could make a small poster for each of the words they investigate, explaining the meaning and how it was arrived at. These can be displayed in the classroom.

- Once children are familiar with the way in which compound words are formed, they could make up some original compound words for familiar objects. Some may be combinations of words which are not yet considered compound words, but which may well become so in the future, for example, *tissue box, petrol station, sports kit*.

- Choose a topic or subject area which uses a variety of compound words and make a collection of all the compound words they can find on the subject (for example, objects to pack in a suitcase, things to do with the seaside and the beach, things connected to school, clothing).

- Use large pictures where either places or multiple objects are shown to find compound words. The pictures in some recent, highly illustrated alphabet books, such as *Animalia* by Graeme Base, could prove rich sources. The NLS (2000) Key Stage 2 Spelling Bank materials suggest using illustrations of a Greek myth for this activity.

Rules and mnemonics

There are very many regularities in English spelling. It has been estimated that around 75% of words are regular and one study states that only 3% of words are so irregular and unpredictable that they have to be learned by rote.

Some of the regularities can usefully be encapsulated in rules or generalisations, though some of the rules prescribed in the past were so difficult to follow that young spellers, who most need the help, would have great difficulty understanding them, for example:

> *Monosyllables and words of more than one syllable with the accent on the last syllable, which end in a single consonant preceded by a single vowel, double the final consonant when adding a suffix beginning with a vowel.*

> *Wheat, 1932*

This is an example of a rule which is difficult to follow and thus not very helpful!

The generalisations which we point out to children should seek to describe what happens as a guide to selecting the appropriate spelling. There are almost always words which are exceptions to a general principle and, when these are encountered, the fact that they do not follow the rule should be noted.

Mike Torbe (1995) suggests that there are a few rules (or descriptions) which work consistently (the examples have been added):

- q *is always followed by* u *and another vowel always follows, for example,* **queen**, **quick**.
- i *(as a long vowel) /ie/ at the end of a word is spelled* y *or (less often)* –igh, *for example,* **sky**, **try**, **fly**, **high**, **sigh**.
- *Words that sound as if they have* o *(as a long vowel) /oe/ in them generally spell it with* oa *in the middle of the word and* ow *at the end, for example,* **boat**, **coat**, **throw**, **follow**.
- *Words that sound as if they have* a *(as a long vowel) /ae/ in them generally spell it* ai *in the middle and* ay *at the end, for example,* **rain**, **plain**, **play**, **say**.
- *English words do not end with* i, ou, u, j *or* v. *Instead they follow these patterns:*

$i = ie$ or $y = $ ***pie***, ***cry***
$ou = ow = $ ***cow***
$u = ue = $ ***blue***
$j = ge$ or $dge = $ ***rage***, ***judge***
$v = ve = $ ***give***
Words which are exceptions (ski *or* raj) *were not English words to start with!*
● *The /*er/ *sound at the end of words is generally spelled* –er, *for example,* bet**ter**, consid**er**.
● *When you add* -full *to the end of a word, it drops one* l *and becomes* –ful, *for example,* beauti**ful**, spoon**ful**.

(pages 77–8)

Torbe gives these as examples of the kinds of generalisations which spellers will be able to make after having had experience of these spelling patterns. He suggests that teachers should help pupils to notice the patterns and then introduce the generalisation. This approach is also found in the NLS (2000) Key Stage 2 Spelling Bank materials, following children's investigations.

Some spelling generalisations

There are some generalisations about principles of spelling which can offer useful guidance. Once children have encountered words which follow a particular principle, the rule can be noted in a spelling notebook or journal, to keep for future revision. Some of these are dealt with in other sections.
1. Principles for adding suffixes (see page 70).
2. Adding plural endings (inflectional suffixes) (see page 80).
3. Contractions (see below).
Other useful generalisations include:

i **before** *e*	**except after** *c*
piece	receive
niece	receipt
priest	deceive
chief	deceit
belief	conceive
thief	conceit
grief	ceiling
brief	
field	
shield	

Some popular names (proper nouns) do not follow this rule; for example, *Sheila, Keith, Neil.* Teachers with classes where children have these names will need to be aware of this when teaching the rule!

Some words in common use in classrooms, with the vowel sound */ae/* or */ie/* also have the *ei* spelling.

/ae/	/ie/
eight	height
eighty	either
eighteen	neither
weight	
neighbour	
reign	

Hard and soft consonant phonemes

The letters *c* and *g* can both be used to represent different phonemes:

The letter *c* can be */k/* or */s/*.
The letter *g* can be */g/* or */j/*.

There is a consistent pattern to this variation. When *c*, either as an initial consonant or within a word is followed by *e, i* or *y*, the sound is soft – */s/*.

Soft *c* – */s/*
circle
cycle
centigrade
century
certain
celery
cell
concentrate
recipe

When the *c* is followed by *a, o* or *u*, then the sound is hard – /k/.

Hard *c* – /k/
cat
cartoon
camera
camel
cord
coffee
colour
cup
curse
cube
cocoon
cucumber

The rule is less consistent for *g*. Whilst there are many words which follow the rule , there are several commonly used words where *g* followed by *i* or *e* has a hard sound – /*g*/:

Soft *g* – /j/	**Hard *g* – /g/**
gentle	game
giant	gang
general	gather
germ	go
generous	gold
geography	gorilla
manager	guest
George	gum
	guide
	girl
	get
	give
	giggle

Mnemonics

The word *mnemonic* originally comes from a Greek word which means *remember*. In English, it means 'designed to aid the memory'.

In spelling, this is usually a phrase highlighting letter combinations or a phrase or sentence using the order of the letters in a word. It is used to help writers remember the spelling.

> sol**di**ers **die**
> there is a **rat** in sepa**rat**e
> have a **pie**ce of **pie**
> one **c**offee with two **s**ugars is ne**cess**ary
> **b**ig **e**lephants **c**an **a**lways **u**nderstand **s**mall **e**lephants – be**cause**

There are some very well-known mnemonics but the most useful tend to be those which have been created by learners, focusing on words or parts of words which they have difficulty with. They are especially helpful for remembering the unstressed vowels or unstressed consonants in words such as:

> vegetable – **get** a **table** for the ve**getable**
> secretary – the keeper of your **secret**
> February – **RU** (are you) ready to spell Feb**ru**ary

The process of creating a mnemonic can be a positive way of learning the spelling of a particular word. Some teachers suggest that children create mnemonics for their personal bank of misspelled words. Sometimes the creation of a class mnemonic, especially a funny one, can serve to help children learn a word:

> **s**ome **c**hildren **h**ave **o**ily **o**range **l**egs – school
> **p**robably **e**very **o**ld **p**erson **l**ikes **e**lephants – people

The National Literacy Strategy places considerable emphasis on helping children to make generalisations from investigations of spelling patterns in words. In order to guide learners into identifying consistent rules, teachers need to be aware of these themselves and to be able to identify possible problems and inconsistencies, especially with commonly quoted rules such as '*i* before *e* except after *c*'.

Why you need to know these facts

- Provide children with spelling notebooks, divided into sections. In these they should record any rules or generalisations they have been taught. They can also be used to record personal spelling lists and reminders about how to set about learning difficult words. Personal or class

Teaching ideas

mnemonics should also be noted for future reference.

- Prepare sets of words with hard *c* sounds and soft *c* sounds. Ask the children to sort these into two sets: a hard *c* set and a soft *c* set.

Ask the children what they notice about the letters following the *c* and then to propose a rule to describe how to remember the spelling of words: with soft *c*, with hard *c*. Include the words *concert* and *concentrate* in the set and ask children what they notice about these two words.

A follow-up to this could be a 'Hard *c*, Soft *c*' Quiz with questions such as:
- Who can think of a word beginning with a hard *c* and ending with a vowel? *(camera)*
- Who can think of a word beginning with a soft *c* which has something to do with a hundred? (for example, *cent, century, centurion, centigrade*)

Extra points should be given if the person giving the word can spell it correctly.

- A similar activity could be devised for *g*, although you need to be aware that there is less consistency.

- Focus on particular spelling patterns for a week at a time and make class posters recording the rule. These should show examples collected during the week.
- Soft *C*s and Hard *C*s
- Irregular plurals
- Adjectives ending in *-ful*

Some posters can be added to over longer periods of time, for example, 'Our class mnemonics for difficult words'.

- Ask children to investigate particular rules to see whether they can find inconsistencies, for example:
- *q* is always followed by *u* in English;
- words that sound as if they have *a* (as long vowel) */ae/* in them are spelled with *ai* in the middle and *ay* at the end.

Contractions, abbreviations and acronyms

Contractions

The spelling of contracted forms of words often poses problems. Sometimes this is because the words are homophones, such as *they're (there, their), we're (wier), who's (whose), he'll (heel), we'll (wheel), aren't (aunt)*.

More often, though, the problem arises in the punctuation of the contraction because children do not understand the principle of something being omitted. *Contractions* are words where two words have been joined together and shortened, with an apostrophe placed where a letter or letters have been left out.

> *cannot / can't.* The apostrophe replaces the omitted *n* and *o*.
> *you are / you're.* The apostrophe replaces the omitted *a*.

It is important to stress to children that the apostrophe marks omission, not the break between the two words.

Contractions appear less frequently in formal written English, but children need to know the correct forms so that they can be used in written speech or dialogue.

Contractions fall into two main groups.

1. Contractions of the *negative* – 'not', as in:

can't	don't	won't	isn't
aren't	didn't	shan't	hadn't
hasn't	doesn't	wasn't	haven't
mustn't	needn't	weren't	couldn't
wouldn't	shouldn't		

The unusual forms of *won't* and *shan't*, where the base word has been modified, should be mentioned.

2. Contractions of *verb forms – am, is, are, will, shall, have, had, would* – as in:

> **am**
> I am   I'm

is

he is, he has	he's
she is, she has	she's
it is	it's
who is	who's
that is	that's
here's	here is
there is	there's

are

we are	we're
you are	you're
who are	who're
they are	they're

will/shall

I will, I shall	I'll
we will, we shall	we'll
he will, he shall	he'll
she will, she shall	she'll
you will, you shall	you'll
who will, who shall	who'll
they will, they shall	they'll

have

I have	I've
we have	we've
you have	you've
they have	they've

had/would

I had, I would	I'd
he had, he would	he'd
we had, we would	we'd
you had, you would	you'd
who had, who would	who'd
they had, they would	they'd

There are a few other forms which children will encounter:

us	let's (let us)
of the	o'clock (of the clock)
it	'tis (it is)
madam	ma'am
them	tell 'em (tell them)

Abbreviations

In the modern world, abbreviations are increasingly used. Some are so frequent that the meaning is conveyed by the abbreviation alone and the original words have been largely forgotten. Many adults will not be able to provide the full version of common abbreviations:

British Broadcasting Corporation	BBC
Independent Television Authority	ITA
International Standard Book Number	ISBN
Very High Frequency	VHF
Her Majesty's Ship	HMS
Department for Education and Employment	DfEE
Teacher Training Agency	TTA
world wide web	www
compact disc	CD
bovine spongiform encephalitis	BSE
unidentified flying object	UFO

Old grammar books often had long lists of abbreviations to be learned. There are now so many of these in common use where the meaning is clearly understood that it is debatable whether it is necessary to know what the abbreviation stands for.

Young people are developing new abbreviations for use in text messages on mobile phones. These are not necessarily abbreviations which use initial letters of the words, although some are:

MYOB –	mind your own business
HAND –	have a nice day

Others represent the sounds of the language, using consonants and numerical symbols, for example, but few vowels (rather like young children's invented spelling!):

WAN2TLK	want to talk
B4	before
LITL	little
TXT MSGS	text messages
M8S	mates
GR8	great
LO	hello

There are now dictionaries of text abbreviations published for text message users.

Acronyms

Some abbreviations have become words in their own right – these are known as *acronyms*. Children will be familiar with many of these and an investigation of those they encounter would be interesting.

laser	**l**ight **a**mplification by the **s**timulated **e**mission of **r**adiation
radar	**ra**dio **d**etection **a**nd **r**anging
Aids	**a**cquired **i**mmune **d**eficiency **s**yndrome
scuba (diving equipment)	**s**elf-**c**ontained **u**nderwater **b**reathing **a**pparatus

Such words have now become so much a part of the language that few will know their source. Good dictionaries would be needed for investigations.

Other acronyms are still generally written with capitals (the initial letters of the words) but are pronounced as words:

UNESCO	**U**nited **N**ations **E**ducational, **S**cientific and **C**ultural **O**rganisation
UNICEF	**U**nited **N**ations **I**nternational **C**hildren's **E**mergency **F**und
NATO	**N**orth **A**tlantic **T**reaty **O**rganisation
SALT	**S**trategic **A**rms **L**imitation **T**alks
INSET	**In** **S**ervice **E**ducation for **T**eachers
OFSTED	**Of**fice for **St**andards in **Ed**ucation
TESOL	**T**eaching **E**nglish to **S**peakers of **O**ther **L**anguages

Many acronyms and abbreviations are known only to those in the field in which they apply. The world of education, for example, is full of these, used amongst teachers but incomprehensible to the uninitiated: EAL, SEN, NLS, ITT, ICT, QCA, NQT, LEA, SAT, SENCO!

You need to know about contractions and the underlying principle of omission, in order to be able to explain this to children. Knowledge of what the term *acronym* means and how this relates to abbreviations will not be drawn on regularly; this will be useful only when explaining about acronym words which are unusual. The word *acronym* is itself one of the group of words you will encounter in talking about language – *antonym, synonym, homonym* – so you will need to understand its meaning.

Teaching ideas

• Play 'Contraction Bingo'. Make a set of boards showing the abbreviated forms of words (contractions). Make a set of cards, showing the full forms of these words. Each set should focus on one group (negatives or verb forms) for that game. The caller reads out the abbreviated forms which players cover on their boards with the appropriate card showing the full form.

• Make a class collection of commercially used abbreviations, which do not necessarily fit within these groups, for example, *pick 'n' mix, mix 'n' match, Toys 'R' Us*. Display these, with explanations of the abbreviation.

• Make a similar collection of abbreviations in common use (for example, BBC, CD, UFO) and provide the unabbreviated forms alongside these. Children could be asked to find these in collaboration with their families, perhaps as homework.

Synonyms and antonyms

Synonyms

Subject facts

The word *synonym* is derived from Greek words meaning *same* and *name*. So, synonyms are words which have the same meaning. In fact, it is not strictly accurate to say that the meanings are exactly the same; in most cases there are slight nuances of meaning or of emphasis which are different.

Sometimes differences lie in the degree of formality of the context or the language:

insane	most formal
mad	slightly less formal
loony/barmy	very informal

Sometimes there is a *regional/dialect* difference. All of the words below describe the making of tea, depending on where the tea is made:

brew	in the northwest, parts of Suffolk, Norfolk & Welsh borders
mash	large areas of northern England, parts of the Midlands and Norfolk
make	the most Standard English form, in the South Midlands, Cambridge area, home counties
draw	south of London and Essex
scald	northwest Welsh border
steep, soak	west of England (Devon, Cornwall, Somerset)

The words are *synonymous,* in the sense that they mean the same, but would be used in different locations.

There are really no perfect synonyms, but in most cases an alternative can be found which is close enough in meaning to be described as a synonym.

enough	sufficient
generous	unstinting/magnanimous
puzzled	perplexed
naughty	mischievous/perverse
kingly	royal
sad	miserable/unhappy
pleased	happy/delighted

The NLS suggests that the use of synonyms adds variety to writing and helps to avoid overuse of the same vocabulary. Certainly children enjoy hunting for new words and should be asked to consider whether alternatives are possible, especially for over-worked adjectives such as *nice, pretty, big, good.* The search for alternatives could provide a context for introducing children to a thesaurus (see page 60).

Antonyms

The word *antonym* is derived from Greek words meaning *opposite* and *name*. So an antonym is a word which has the opposite meaning from another word. The words must be seen as pairs which have opposite meanings.

black/white	clean/dirty
high/low	first/last
far/near	dark/light

With children, teachers generally refer to opposites and there is often a straightforward, easily perceived sense of converseness in pairs of words. When the question 'What is the opposite of X?' is asked, we know that the answer is going to be 'Y'.

What is the opposite of *wet*	*(dry)*
What is the opposite of *big*	*(little)*
What is the opposite of *empty*	*(full)*
What is the opposite of *over*	*(under)*
What is the opposite of *buy*	*(sell)*

The majority of words in the language do not have an opposite – there is no antonym for *tree, coffee, cat or sandwich.* You could not ask the question 'What is the opposite of?' of any of these.

Many antonyms are created by the addition of a prefix *(un-, dis-, mis-, de-, anti-):*

happy	unhappy
agree	disagree
behave	misbehave
activate	deactivate
clockwise	anticlockwise
logical	illogical

See also pages 68–9 for more on prefixes.

Word structure and spelling conventions

Antonym pairs often occur close together in writing, either in the same sentence or following very closely. Some children's authors exploit this in entertaining ways.

> **Simpkin (Quentin Blake)**
> Simpkin high, Simpkin low,
> Simpkin fast, Simpkin slow.

> **Titch (Pat Hutchins)**
> 'Mary had a big bike. Tich had a little tricycle.'
> 'Pete had a big drum. And Titch had a little wooden whistle.'

• Make sets of cards for antonym pairs, each word on a separate card. Mix these up and ask children to sort them into the correct pairs. A variation of this could be to place all cards face down and to play a 'Pelmanism' or 'Pairs' game, where children take turns to turn over two cards. If they make an antonym pair, the two cards are retained. If the two are not a pair, they are turned back over. The ultimate aim is to remember where the cards are placed to find the pairs.

• Select an antonym and ask children to suggest synonyms for this.

unhappy	miserable, sad
unwell	ill, sick, poorly
small	tiny, minute, titchy

This could be a group activity, using dictionaries.

• Point out that antonyms are often used close together in written texts. Ask the class to look for antonym pairs, either in their reading of shared texts, or in group reading activities.

• Make class collections of synonyms, especially for overused words.

nice	pretty, handsome, attractive, appealing, beautiful, pleasing, pleasant, agreeable, kind, friendly, considerate, delightful

Ask children to compose some sentences using each of the synonyms and then discuss the slight differences in meaning and emphasis. This could be a group activity, followed by whole-class discussion of the meanings. Dictionaries of synonyms could be used.

• Give groups of children words with the potential for finding synonyms. Each group uses a thesaurus to locate synonyms and compiles a group list. These could be made into class posters.

Resources

References and further reading
Crystal, D (1995) *The Cambridge Encylopedia of the English Language,* Cambridge: Cambridge University Press
Crystal, D (1987) *The Cambridge Encylopedia of Language,* Cambridge: Cambridge University Press
National Literacy Strategy Framework for Teaching (1998), London: DfEE
National Literacy Strategy (1999) *Progression in Phonics,* London: DfEE
National Literacy Strategy (2000) *Spelling Bank,* London: DfEE
Torbe, M (1995) *Teaching and Learning Spelling,* East Grinstead: Ward Lock Educational
Wheat, LB (1932) 'Four Spelling Rules' in *Elementary School Journal* xxxii, pp 679–706

Children's books
Ahlberg, Janet & Allan (1982) *The Ha-Ha Bonk Book,* Harmondsworth: Puffin Books
Base, G (1986) *Animalia,* Harmondsworth: Puffin Books
Blake, Q (1993) *Simpkin,* London: Jonathan Cape
Hutchins, P (1974) *Titch,* Harmondsworth: Puffin Books
The Crack a Joke Book (1978 – in aid of Oxfam), Harmondsworth: Puffin Books (old, but may be available in school libraries)

ICT resources

Fun School Spelling, Europress for DOS and on CD for PC

I Hate Spelling, Dorling Kindersley

My First Incredible Amazing Dictionary, Dorling Kindersley
CD-ROM (Win/Mac)

Starspell (1999), Fisher-Marriott Software

Other classroom spelling resources

See Chapter 4 for details of several dictionaries.

Wordbanks related to topics being studied

Collection of joke books, especially focusing on puns

Teacher-made card games

– 'Pairs'/'Pelmanism'

– for prefix/root matching

– for root/suffix matching

– opposites (antonyms)

– contraction matching

– synonyms

Old newspapers and magazines and highlighter pens for
word searches of different kinds

Chapter 4

History and the English language

The English language is a fascinating subject of study in its own right. Word study does not have to be dry or tedious – there is much that is fascinating and entertaining which children enjoy finding out. This chapter looks at some of the history of the English language and factors which have influenced both the vocabulary we use and the spelling of the words. This field of study is called *etymology*, which means 'the study of the history and origin of words'.

The development of the language we speak now can be traced back through written evidence of the languages which were the foundations of the English language. It is as we know it because of invasions and settlements of the British Isles over about 1500 years – from 400BC to AD1066.

Children often enjoy becoming 'word detectives' and the development of an interest in words has been shown to have a positive effect on spelling. Discovery of the reasons for apparently idiosyncratic spellings helps children to remember them.

Sections in this chapter look chronologically at the influences and how these have impacted on our vocabulary and spelling.

The Celts, Old English and the Vikings

Subject facts

The Celts

The Celts were one of many tribes living in Europe in the years before Christ. About 400BC some Celts from Northern France and from the Netherlands crossed the Channel and settled in England, Wales and Scotland. The dialect these people spoke was *Brythonic* and they were known as *Brythons*, from which we get *Britons*. Other Celts from Southern France settled in Ireland and kept their own dialect, now called *Gaelic*. The Celtic influence can still be seen in a few placenamesthroughout the British Isles, where we can find Celtic words for features of the landscape, for example:

afon/avon (river)	as in Avon, Avonmouth, Stratford-upon-Avon
cumm (deep valley)	as in Cumrew, Cumwhitton
penn (hill)	as in Pencraig, Penge, Pendleton, Torpenhow
ros/rhos (rough moorland)	as in Ross, Rossington
creic (rock, cliff)	as in Crick, Creake, Creaton

Many of the placenameswhich have Celtic words in them are located in particular areas (Wales, Cornwall, Cumberland and southwest Scotland) because of later invasions of Romans and Angles, Saxons and Jutes, from whom the Celts moved as far away as possible, finally settling on the edges of Britain.

Roman occupation (55BC/AD43)

The Romans had begun to attack Britain during the first century BC. In AD43 Britain was conquered and became part of the Roman Empire. The Romans ruled Britain until AD410 but remained remarkably separate from the Britons. They built roads and travelled throughout Britain and we can tell where they went from the remains of their building and from a few placenames which were adopted and slightly changed by later invaders.

The Latin word *castra* (OE *ceaster*) was adopted by the Britons and later the Anglo-Saxons. It survives in place-names, for example, Chester, Lancaster, Manchester,

Chichester, Gloucester, Worcester. The total number of Latin words already in English at the beginning of the Anglo-Saxon period was small (linguists estimate no more than 200). Although Latin must have continued for some years, it did not take root in Britain at this time.

Angles, Saxons and Jutes

Starting in AD449, tribes who spoke a Germanic dialect of the Celtic language – the Angles, Saxons and Jutes – invaded and settled. These people became known as the Anglo-Saxons and they gave the name of *Englaland* to their new home; they and their language were *Englisc*. From this, we get *England* and *English*. They called the Britons *wealas* (which meant foreigners!) and it is from this that we have *Wales*. Over a period of nearly 350 years the Anglo-Saxons made England their own and created seven kingdoms whose names still survive: Wessex (West Saxons), Essex (East Saxons), Sussex (South Saxons), East Anglia (mainly Angles), Mercia (mainly Angles), Kent (mainly Jutes) and Northumbria (the land north of the Humber, mainly Angles). Almost all the surviving Celtic placenames were changed to names using their own language. This language we now know as Old English (in dictionary derivations this is abbreviated to OE). Some Old English words are commonly found in placenames today:

ham (homestead, village)	as in Birmingham, Finglesham, Hamstead
ingas (follower of)	as in Finningham, Godalming, Terrington
ton/tun (enclosure, farmstead, village)	as in Thropton, Tunworth, Carsington, Pirton
wic (dairy farm or camp)	as in Chiswick, Wicklewood, Wix, Giggleswick
burh and ceaster (fortress, walled town, fortified place)	as in Newbury, Denbury, Casterton, Leicester

Old English

We know a good deal about Old English vocabulary and word forms because writing from that time has survived. Some was written in the runic alphabet. The Old English verb *writan*, from which we get *write*, means 'to scratch runes into bark'. Other writing, done by monks, used the Roman alphabet. Perhaps the most significant document in

Old English is the *Anglo-Saxon Chronicle*, which is an historical record of the events in Britain from the arrival of the Angles, Saxons and Jutes in 449, through six centuries. The events were actually written down over a period of some 300 years and because this was such a long period, the *Chronicle* records the changes which took place in the language over that time as well.

Many unusual spellings in modern English have their roots in Old English.

wh words

Many of the words we now spell with *wh* were once spelled with *hw*. The spelling change came much later, during the Middle English period, with the influence of French scribes. These include the interrogative words:

Old English	Modern English
hwaet	what
hwaer	where
hwanne/ hwenne	when
hwaether	whether
hwilc	which
hwa	who
hwi/ hwy	why

It also includes many other familiar *wh* words:

Old English	Modern English
hwit	white
hwael	whale
hwaete	wheat
hweo(go)l	wheel
hwearf	wharf

A few others, which originally had only *h* at the beginning, had a *w* added later, probably by Norman French scribes attempting to impose order and keep a pattern found in *th-* and *ch-*.

Old English	Modern English
hal	whole
halsum	wholesome

Words with -ght and -gh

The consonant sound *-gh* in these words would have been pronounced in Old English. The unusual spelling remains even though this sound is no longer vocalised. The Old English words were written with only an *h* which was pronounced (a sound similar to the Scottish pronunciation of *loch*). The *g* was added later to the spelling (again by Norman French scribes) to represent the spoken sound more accurately. We no longer pronounce this *gh* sound in these words but spelling changes which indicated the pronunciation have remained. This leaves us with this consonant trigraph (*-igh*) representing */ie/* and an apparently illogical spelling.

Old English	Modern English
miht/mieht	might
mihtig	mighty
riht	right
sihth	sight
leoht/liht	light
niht/neaht	night
feoht(e)	fight

This spelling is also found in the irregular past tenses of some verbs:

Old English	Modern English
(bringan) brohte	(bring) brought
(thencan) thoht	(think) thought
(secan) sohte	(seek) sought
(agan) ahte	(owe) ought

Words which end with *-gh* have similar roots:

Old English	Modern English
thurh	through
thuruh	thorough
toh	tough
boh	bough
ploh	plough
cowhe	cough
(a Middle English spelling)	

So do a few words which have -*gh*- in the middle.

Old English	Modern English
dohtor	daughter
slahter	slaughter

Silent letters

The existence of some 'silent' letters in the correct modern spelling of words in English is because these letters once represented sounds which are no longer pronounced in the words.

SILENT *W*

In many Old English words beginning with *wr-*, both the /*w*/ and the /*r*/ were pronounced. These included:

wraeth (wrath)	wryhta (wright, as in wheelwright)
wrecan (wreak)	wringan (wring)
writan (write)	gewrinklod (wrinkled)
wrang (wrong)	writhan (writhe)
wrenna (wren)	wrigian (wry)
wraestlian (wrestle)	wrencan (wrench)

SILENT *K*

In Old English words beginning with *cn-*, both the /*k*/ and the /*n*/ were pronounced. The *c* represented a hard /*k*/ sound in the original and so the words came to be spelled with *k* as a more accurate representation of that sound. These included:

cnafa (knave)	cnedan (knead)
cneo (knee)	cnyll (knell)
cnif (knife)	cniht (knight)
cnyttan (knit)	cnocian (knock)
cnotta (knot)	cnawan (know)

In both of these cases the pronunciation of the two consonants together was awkward and so the first was gradually dropped. The spelling, however, retains the redundant letter.

The Vikings

The Vikings were from Scandinavia (Danes and Norwegians) and after much fighting they eventually settled to live alongside the English. Their language, Old Norse, had the same Germanic roots as English, so the two languages merged quite successfully. The most obvious legacy of the Viking settlement is in place-names, in which Old Norse words are easily identifiable.

thorpe	farm or small village (Scunthorpe)
stoke	holy place or monastery (Stoke-on-Trent)
toft	the site of a house and out-buildings (Lowestoft)
by	village or homestead (Derby, Rugby, Whitby)
thwaite	meadow or fenced-off land (Bassenthwaite, Braithwaite)

There are many of these placenames in the northeast of England because the area north of the Midlands (Rugby) and including East Anglia became the *Danelaw*, a kingdom separate from the areas to the south and west, which was ruled by the Danes.

Some Norse words have survived alongside the Old English, often becoming alternatives or synonyms.

skirt (Norse)	shirt (Old English)
anger (Norse)	wrath (Old English)
sick (Norse)	ill (Old English)
skin (Norse)	hide (Old English)
dike (Norse)	ditch (Old English)
skill (Norse)	craft (Old English)

Most Old Norse words died out, but some common words remained and have become part of the English language in use today.

leg, flat, let, get, keel, die, egg, sky, ill, root, neck, want

Many of the English words beginning with the *sk* sound, spelt either *sk* or *sc* are of Norse origin.

History and the English language

skirt	scare	scab
sky	scowl	scale
skin	scant	scruff
skill	scrap	

When exploring these consonant blends, it would be interesting to look up the origins of the words found.

Why you need to know these facts

In order to explain these unusual spellings to children, teachers need to be aware themselves of the history. Many of the most common words still used in English come directly from Old English and many have their spelling and pronunciation unchanged. Others have changed slightly because pronunciation has changed but the spelling reflects older accents. The spelling patterns we now use have their origins in the history of English and some knowledge of the story will help children remember them.

Amazing facts

Many of the single word prepositions in English are Old English words, with the same meaning that they had over 1000 years ago. In some there are slight spelling changes.

in	at (aet)
under	over (ofer)
on	down (dune)
to	by (by)
before (beforan)	behind (behindan)
up (uppan)	
after (aefter)	

Teaching ideas

● Make a timeline to show the dates of invasions into England, the people and the languages they brought. Start with the Celts in 400BC through to the Norman Invasion in AD1066. Show some words which come from each era.

● Combine historical study of a particular period (Romans, Anglo-Saxons and Vikings are common topics in primary schools), with language study. Search for words which came into English at this particular time.

- Older children could undertake research into King Alfred and his kingdom. The Anglo-Saxon Chronicle, the source of much of our knowledge about both events and the language at this time, was probably initiated by King Alfred, the most famous Anglo-Saxon king, reigning in Wessex from 849–99. He arranged for many Latin works to be tranlsated, though most of the surviving Old English texts were written in the period following his reign. As a follow-up look at a children's retelling of *Beowulf*. (See Kevin Crossley-Holland's retelling illustrated by Charles Keeping.)

- Use versions of the Lord's Prayer (a short text) written in Old English, Middle English and Modern English. (See Resources on page 139 for books where this is provided.) Ask children to compare these and to look at the changes which have taken place in the spellings of words.

- Use copies of maps of England (large-scale versions of a small area are the most useful because they have names of villages which are often ancient) and ask children to locate placenameswhich have either Celtic, Anglo-Saxon or Norse words in them. If you prepare mini-dictionaries giving the meanings of the old words, children will be able to translate the place-name, and describe what it originally was like.

- Make spelling lists of *-gh* words, *wh-* words or *sk-/sc-* words and lists of words with a silent *w* or *k* and ask children to use the etymological information in good dictionaries to find the origins. This is a useful exercise for familiarising children with etymological dictionary entries and with dictionary abbreviations such as OE, ME, ON, as well as for developing vocabulary.

The Romans, Christianity and Latin influences

At the same time that the Anglo-Saxon kingdoms and, later, the Vikings, were establishing themselves, Christianity from Rome was spreading throughout the British Isles. The use of Latin by monks producing beautiful manuscripts led to the wider introduction of the Roman alphabet. By 650AD Christianity was established throughout the country and with it came a host of new words. The Latin language provided the basis for thousands of words and parts of words which were added to the existing English.

Subject facts

Latin	Old English	Modern English
altar	alter	altar
candela	candel	candle
missa	maesse	mass
nonna	nunne	nun
presbyter	preost	priest
templum	templ	temple
discipulus	discipul	disciple
abbadissa	abudesse	abbess
vinum	win	wine
angelus	angel	angel

In order to make the Bible more accessible to English Christians, monks began to translate it from Latin into English, which often did not have an appropriate word, so the Latin words were used instead.

Latin prefixes
One of the most lasting influences of Latin has been the prefixes used in English to create new words and change meaning. Though they are dealt with here, many were not used in English until much later (15th and 16th centuries) when there was fresh importation of Latin and Greek words (see pages 130–1 for Greek prefixes) to express new ideas.

Teaching ideas

Prefix	Latin	Meaning	Example
inter-	inter	between	international
sub-	sub	under	submerge
dec(e/i)-	decem	ten	decimal
oct(o)-	octo	eight	octave
bi-	bi	two/twice	bicycle
uni-	unus	one	unicorn
cent-	centum	hundred	century
mini-	minimus	least	minimal
circ(um)-	circum	round/about	circumference
com-/co-	com	with/jointly	combine, co-operate
manu-	manus	hand	manufacture
multi-	multus	much/many	multilingual
non-	non	not	non-stop
omni-	omnis	all	omnivorous
ultra-	ultra	beyond/extreme	ultrasonic

The Latin roots of English words often provide clues to meaning, so it is worth pointing these out to children as a source of information. The NLS Spelling Bank (2000) materials contain several activities to do with prefix meanings so teachers will need sound background knowledge in order to explain these to children. Exploration of families of words having the same prefix will help develop children's vocabulary.

The church also had a strong influence on everyday life and many words for clothing, food and household items were borrowed from Latin, *cap, silk, chest, pear, radish, cell, lily, plant, master, purple, tunic.*

Some of this new vocabulary was a variation on an Old English word, for example:

cap – caeppe (OE) and Latin *cappa – hood;*
pear – pere (OE) and Latin *pirum – pear.*

All the other words in this example represent the many new things, concepts and artefacts which were now appearing in everyday life, all of which had to be named, hence the Latin borrowings.

- Make prefix webs for the most common prefixes. Provide a template for children with the prefix at the centre and ask children to search for words which have this prefix and to write them around it. The meanings of the words should be added so that the consistency of the meaning of the prefix becomes apparent.

Some prefixes lend themselves particularly well to this activity as there are many words to be found, as shown in the example below.

sub-	subway
	submarine
	subcontinent
	subconscious
	substandard
	submerge
	subsoil
	subculture
	subtract

• Make sets of cards of different colours; one set should have prefixes on them, the other should have the meanings. Initially, ask children to match the pairs and to enter these into a spelling notebook (see page 97).

The cards can also be used to play a 'Pelmanism' or 'Pairs' game. All cards are placed face down on a table and children take turns to turn over one of each colour. If the prefix and the meaning match, the player keeps that pair – if not, the cards are put face down again. The aim is to remember where the matched prefix and meaning pairs are located in order to collect as many as possible.

• Investigate vocabulary to do with the church and its services, scholarship and literacy and find out how many are derived from Latin words.

Make collections of these.

• Combine work on historical topics (Romans, the growth of Christianity) with work in English, focusing on vocabulary which comes from Latin roots.

The Normans (French)

The last invasion of the British Isles in 1066 brought French to influence the English language. The Normans defeated the English King Harold and they ruled England for the next 200 years. The people in power in the country spoke only French and a huge gap grew between the upper classes, who used French, and the ordinary people, who spoke only English.

In the 200 years of French rule there was very little writing in English; Latin was used as a common language when the English and their Norman French rulers could not understand each other. Gradually, between 1066 and 1500 thousands of new words entered the language from French, and English became much more like modern English. The assimilation of changes to the language took time and the period between the 12th and 15th century was the time of Middle English, the language in which the poet Chaucer wrote *The Canterbury Tales*.

Some words from Old English survived alongside the French to give us synonyms or alternatives with a slightly different meaning:

Old English roots	French roots
yearly	annual
might	power
smell	odour
ask	question
kingly	royal
child	infant
book	volume
doom	judgement
house	mansion
freedom	liberty
happiness	felicity
help	aid
hide	conceal
tongue	language
wedding	marriage
wish	desire
holy	saintly
sorrow	grief

Not surprisingly, at this time very many words associated with ruling the country entered the language. These can be categorised:

Administration
authority, bailiff, constable, court, government, mayor, parliament, revenue, tax, treaty

Law
accuse, arrest, blame, crime, evidence, fine, jail, judge, jury, punishment, prison

Military
army, battle, captain, barbican, combat, enemy, defeat, guard, navy, soldier, peace

There were also words many associated with food and drink, fashion, the arts, science, learning and the home. Amongst the most well known are the words given to meat:

Old English	French
ox	beef (boeuf)
sheep	mutton (mouton)
calf	veal (veau)
deer	venison (venaison)
pig/swine	pork (porc)
fowl	poultry (pouleterie)

The existence of the parallel words has led to the use of those derived from French for the food and those derived from Old English for the animal.

After the Norman conquest, French scribes brought the spelling patterns of written French to words which were English.

The /k//w/ sound in Old English had been spelled with *cw*-; in French, it was *qu*-. Thus the *qu*- spelling appeared in English words:

Old English spelling	New spelling
cwic	quick
cwen	queen
cwell	quell
cwacian	quake
cwencan	quench

Many other *qu*- words are derived from French in which this spelling pattern existed:
quality, question, qualify, quail, quantity, quarrel, quarter, quest, quiet.

The *hw*- spelling of Old English was also changed to *wh*- by French scribes, to match the *th*- spelling pattern (see page 112).

French affixes
Many prefixes and suffixes used to construct abstract terms came into English at this time.

These included:

Affix	Meaning	Examples
con-	with, together	conform, conclude, concede, conduct
trans-	across	transcribe, transcend, transfer, transport
pre-	before	preface, prelude, preclude, precondition
-a(e)nce	'state of'	annoyance, perseverance, obedience
-(t)ion	'act of'	perfection, direction, inhibition, creation
-ment	makes noun from verb	contentment, government, judgement

Why you need to know these facts

The French influence on English, started by the Norman invasion, has been considerable. The impact of the assimilation of so much new vocabulary changed English in an important way. It has been estimated that some 10,000 French words came into English at that time. Old English forms became fewer and what we know as Middle English is very much closer to modern English. Investigation of some of the changes and the reasons for them can help children remember spellings and also develop understanding of a wider vocabulary.

Amazing facts

There are very many words in French and English which look the same or nearly the same. Although the pronunciation is different, an English speaker would be able to understand the written French word.

English	French
village	village
transport	transport
preface	preface
conform	conforme
direction	direction
creation	creation
transcription	transcription
government	gouvernement

History and the English language

- Collect sets of synonyms and set up investigations of these to discover the origins of the words. Older children, especially if they are studying French, could be asked to find the French words which those with French roots have come from. The investigations will promote the use of etymological entries in dictionaries and familiarisation with the abbreviations used (OE, OF, ME).

- Investigate prefixes and suffixes used to create abstract ideas. Many of these will be abstract nouns.

    Give the children a set of verbs and ask them to add suffixes to create nouns. The *-ion* suffix may be preceded by *s* as well as *t*. Look at where letters must be dropped to add the suffix and formulate a rule or generalisation.

Verb	Noun
direct	direction
promote	promotion
complete	completion
educate	education
reduce	reduction
translate	translation
produce	production
extend	extension
confuse	confusion
explode	explosion
erode	erosion
collide	collision
discuss	discussion
possess	possession
oppress	oppression
profess	profession

A similar activity could be carried out using the *-ment* and *-ance/-ence* suffixes.

- Collect vocabulary to do with government, the law, religion, and investigate the origins of the words. Are there any terms or titles which come from Old English?

- Collect vocabulary to do with food and cooking. There is a very strong French influence in this field though much of the vocabulary has come into English at later periods, for example, café, restaurant, dessert.

The beginning of Standard English and printing

As the Normans began to lose their power in the 13th century, the use of French decreased and English began to be used again in government and for writing literature. At this time there were six main regional varieties of Middle English, and writing in different parts of the country used different vocabulary, grammar and pronunciation. As English was used more and more for official documents there began the move towards a common written form of the language.

A written Standard English began to emerge in the 15th century. One dialect, that of the East Midlands, an area bounded by a triangle formed by the two major universities, Oxford and Cambridge, and London, the seat of power, acquired a higher status than the others. Modern linguists argue that extensive migration from the Central Midlands (Leicestershire, Northamptonshire and Bedfordshire) to London also influenced the London dialect. Even at this time there were those who looked down upon dialect forms from other regions and when the first Grammar books were written in the 14th and 15th centuries, the grammar of this high status southern/London dialect came to be seen as 'more correct' (see Chapter 5 for more on dialects).

When William Caxton (see Appendix) first started printing books he had to consider which variety of English he should use, given that there were major regional differences at this time. His press was situated in London where there were many asserting the superiority of the southern dialect, so it was inevitable that this would be the variety he chose.

Spelling

Spelling, too, began to be more standardised with the advent of printing in 1476 when William Caxton set up his printing press in Westminster.

Until the advent of print the spelling choices of scribes and scriveners had been largely personal. Generally words were assigned letters which represented the sounds which could be heard. Caxton's decisions brought some standardisation of spelling as well as dialect, but also introduced some of his own idiosyncratic spellings. Some of these related to representation of sounds in words; others related to layout and line length in the printing.

Gh

One reason for this letter combination was the search for a way of representing the Old English /h/ sound (see page 113). Another reason was Caxton's decision to spell the English hard /g/ with *gh-*. He had been trained as a printer in the Netherlands and probably adopted this letter combination from Flemish to represent the hard /g/. A very few words had the spelling changed:

gast	became	ghost
gastly	became	ghastly
gurkyn	became	gherkin

Floating e/ silent e

It had been proposed by Richard Mulcaster (a 16th century teacher and scholar who had written books on spelling; see Appendix) that the addition of an *e* at the end of one-syllable words with a long vowel in them would enable pupils to distinguish these words. This advice was acted upon, but not consistently, especially by printers who tended to add letters in order to justify lines of print. This may explain the number of words which had an *e* added, even though the vowel was a short vowel, for example, *some, come, gone, done, give, love, dove, glove, have.*

The practice of justification (making a line fit between straight left and right margins) meant adding letters, especially the additional *e*. In printed texts one could, therefore, find a range of spellings of the same word, even in the same text:

dog	dogg	dogge
been	beene	
booke	boke	
had	hadde	
axed	axyd (asked)	

By the end of the 16th century there was growing standardisation of both dialect and orthography. Richard Mulcaster had been one whose views had influenced and fostered standardisation of spelling. Several aspects of spelling became more predictable:

- There was increased use of doubled vowels (for example, *oo, ee*) to indicate a long vowel.

- The silent *e* at the end of a syllable was used to indicate a long vowel sound (for example, *hope, save*).

- A doubled consonant within a word indicated a preceding short vowel (for example, *sitting, letter*).

- There was still some confusion about what happened at the end of a word having a short vowel preceding a consonant (for example, *well* but *wet; glass* but *glad*). This inconsistency has persisted in modern spelling.

Why you need to know these facts

Knowledge about the history of both the gradual standardisation of the accepted dialect and the spelling system of English provides a useful background for giving explanations to children. Most children like to know how curious spellings arose and are usually fascinated by the varied spellings of words in the past. Stories about real people (for example, Caxton and Mulcaster) provide a good context for exploring particular spelling patterns.

Amazing facts

Even highly literate people spelled words differently on different occasions. Spelling was so unpredictable in the past that people often wrote their own names in different ways at different times.

The much quoted example is that of William Shakespeare who spelled his name in a variety of different ways between 1612 and 1616. These are set out in the example below:

> Shakspe(r)
> Shakp(er)
> Shaksper
> Shakspere
> Shakspeare
>
> (The brackets show letters which appear to be missing.)

History and the English language

- Ask children to investigate words with *gh-* spellings at the beginning. An etymological dictionary will show which came from Old English and will give the OE word. Several other *gh-* words come from other languages, notably Hindi.

- Ask older children to find out about William Caxton and the start of printing. Use information texts about the period to gather information about him, his press and the kinds of books he produced. Many scribes and scriveners were fiercely opposed to printing – ask children why might that be. A children's historical novel, *A Load of Unicorn* by Cynthia Harnett would be of interest here. It tells of the rivalry between Caxton and the scriveners and the central child character is Caxton's apprentice!

- Provide a list of words related to book publishing and ask children to research the meanings of these: scribe, scrivener, illuminator, bookbinder, manuscript, stationer, upper case/lower case letters.

- Ask children to collect sets of words spelled with a silent *e* at the end. Make a set for the single vowels *a, i, o, u* (but not *e* because there are few words with *e–e*).

a–e	i–e	o–e	u–e
make	rise	hole	use
take	life	home	cure
have (short)	give(short)	bone	cube
safe	hide	nose	mule
rage	pipe	note	flute
cape	ice	love(short)	tune

Once collected, classify these into:
   i) those with a long vowel sound and those with a short vowel sound. Are there any *u–e* words which have a short vowel sound?
   ii) the rime families (see page 29) for each vowel.

-abe	-ake	-ate	-ace	-ale
-afe	-ave	-ade	-ame	-aze
-ase	-age	-ape		

The Renaissance, trade and exploration

During the 16th century there was a renewed interest in the classical languages and literature as well as in the new fields of learning, science, medicine and the arts. Before this time the language of learning and scholarship was Latin, but there now came numerous publications in English. Many of these were translations so the translators used thousands of Latin and Greek terms because there was no equivalent vocabulary in English. The effect of this interest in new ideas on the English language was extensive and far-reaching. The vocabulary grew, incorporating new words to express new concepts and inventions. Most of these were taken from Latin and Greek, though there were also many from French, Italian, Spanish and Portuguese.

Subject facts

This was also the time of world-wide exploration and trade so vocabulary from other languages was imported along with the goods.

There was then, as now, considerable debate and resistance from some purists regarding the assimilation of foreign vocabulary, but this did not stop the influx of the new words.

Words for plants, products and artefacts
There were very large numbers of these. The source is shown after the word.

cocoa (Spanish)	macaroni (Italian)
chocolate (French)	rocket (Italian)
tomato (French)	canoe (Spanish)
potato (Spanish)	guitar (Spanish)
tobacco (Spanish)	tank (Spanish)
anchovy (Spanish)	knapsack (Dutch)
apricot (Spanish)	stiletto (Italian)
hoist (Dutch)	umbrella (Italian)
banana (Spanish)	yacht (Dutch)
maize (Spanish)	boom (Dutch)
port /wine (Spanish)	spool(Dutch)
sombrero (Spanish)	easel (Dutch)
hammock (Spanish)	deck (Dutch)
passport (French)	battery (French)
vase (French)	groove(Dutch)

Words associated with music and the arts

As one might expect, many of these came from Italian.

balcony	opera
cameo	solo
carnival	sonata
concerto	sonnet
cupola	soprano
design	stanza
grotto	stucco
violin	piano
portico	design

Words associated with science and medicine

Most of these came from Latin and Greek.

delirium	disability
epilepsy	external
glottis	larynx
pancreas	parasite
pneumonia	skeleton
species	system
temperature	tendon
thermometer	tibia
virus	tonic
ulna	atmosphere
catastrophe	chaos
contradictory	criterion
critic	exaggerate
extinguish	lunar
obstruction	inclemency
vacuum	

Greek prefixes

It was at this time that much Greek vocabulary began to be used, both as prefixes and to create new terms. These have continued to be appropriated whenever new ideas needed to be expressed.

Much modern technological terminology uses Greek words.

Prefix	Greek	Meaning	Example
ex-	ex	out/forth	exclude
anti-	anti	against	antibiotic
auto	autos	self	autobiography
chromo	khroma	colour	chromatic
hemi	hemi	half	hemisphere
hydro-	hudro	water	hydrometer
hyper-	huper	over/beyond	hypersensitive
hypo-	hupo	under/below	hypothermia
mega-	megas	great	megaphone
micro-	mikros	small	microscope
mono-	monos	single/one	monosyllable
photo-	photos	light	photograph
poly-	polus	much/many	polysyllabic
pseudo-	pseudes	false	pseudonym
tele-	tele	far off	telephone
techno-	tekhne	art	technology

If we look at the words listed under Examples it becomes very clear that these words make use of other Greek words. In fact, often, the word has been derived entirely from Greek. Many are examples of words created because no word existed to name a new concept.

autobiography (writing the story of one's own life)
auto (self)
-bio (human life – Greek: bios)
-graphy (things written – Greek: graphos)

hydrometer (instrument for determining the density of liquids)
hydro (water)
-meter (measuring instrument –Greek: metron)

megaphone (speaking instrument for sending sound of voice over a distance)
mega (great)
-phone (sound – Greek: phone)

technology (science of practical or industrial art(s))
techno (art)
-logy (the study of – Greek: logia)

It is possible to break down a great many words in this way and thus to reveal their meanings. Any of these elements used in other words retains a consistent meaning, so we know, for example, that a word with *-ology* at the end is about the study of something; a word with *bio-* in it has something to do with life; a word with *-phone* in it has to do with sound. Once some of these Greek roots are known, it is possible to analyse and understand the meanings of new words. Older pupils can be shown how to do this. Recent words created for new artefacts are a rewarding source for this kind of analysis.

Silent *p* words

Another silent letter in English is *p* at the beginning of a word. These words also come from Greek, for example, *psychology,* the study of the mind, comes from the Greek *psukhe* (soul, spirit, mind – see the Greek myth of Psyche and Eros) and *-logy* (see above).

Similar words include *psychic, psychedelic, psychiatry, psychoanalysis, psychopath, psychosomatic, psychometric, psychological.*

Pneumonia, an infection of the lungs; comes from the Greek *pneuma* (wind)/*pneo* (breathe), *-ia* a suffix, also from Greek, used to form a noun. The only other *pn-* words are related to either the word *pneumonia* or the word *pneumatic.*

Because of the Greek roots, the spelling of these words in English retains the *p,* although it is not pronounced.

Why you need to know these facts

The influence of other languages, especially Greek, on English hugely increased the vocabulary of the language. It is interesting to know where foreign words come from and essential to understand the way in which Greek and Latin affixes and base words combine to create new meanings. Work in this area will not only develop children's vocabulary and spelling skills, but also provides a fascinating field for investigation and detective work on words. Teachers' own knowledge is important if children are to be supported and guided in this.

Amazing facts

Silent *b* words

It was at this time that the letter *b* was added to some Middle English words to make them look like Latin words. This was probably simply a case of scholars showing off their knowledge of Latin, but gives us two instances of a *b* in the middle of a word which is not pronounced, shown in the following example:

dette (ME) became *debt* (Latin: *debitum*) so we also have
debtor (but *debit* – in which the *b* is pronounced)
doute (ME) became *doubt* (Latin: *dubitare*) so we also have
doubting, doubted, doubtful, doubtfully, doubtless

Teaching ideas

• Give children a list of foods (especially fruits and
vegetables) and ask them to find out where they came from
originally. They will need etymological dictionaries to find
out the language the word came from. Then they will need
to consider why the word we use came from that language
(explorers, grown in that country).

This could also be done for musical terms or for
architecture and art. Why would the words we use have
originated in those countries?

• Collect sets of words with particular Greek prefixes and
ask children to look up the meanings.

telephone	microscope	automatic
telegraph	microphone	autobiography
telescope	microcomputer	automation
television	microbe	autograph
telephoto	microfilm	autopilot
telegramme	microwave	autocycle
telepathy	microsurgery	automaton
telecommunication	micro-electronics	automobile
teleprinter	microcosm	

Many of these words will have other elements of Greek
origin. Get the children to consider why this might be so
(new ideas, products without names, for example,
microcomputer, microwave).

• Make class collections of all the words children can find
with *-ology* in them. What do they mean? (Good dictionaries
will be important for this.) The same can be done for several
other Greek elements: *bio, phone, graphy, scope, kilo-, syn-*.

• If the Tudors are a history topic, look at the routes
explorers and merchants (English, Spanish, Portuguese,
Italian) took and link this work with language study of
foreign words assimilated into English.

- Similarly, look at the immigration, especially of Dutch workers, into England and at the jobs immigrants did which brought new words into the language (weavers, printers, workers in the Fens, artists).

Modern English to world English

Subject facts

Since the days of exploration in the 15th and 16th centuries, Britain has continued to be a major trading nation. The British were also once colonisers and builders of a huge British Empire. Whatever the effects of colonization in political, economic and human terms, the linguistic effect was the growth of the English language across the whole world.

In one sense this was a two-way process, with much vocabulary from around the world becoming a part of the English lexicon. These new words are often described as *loan words* or *borrowings,* though this is not really an accurate description as the words are not given back! English has always been a voracious borrower of words from other languages. It has been estimated that there are words from more than 120 different languages in our present-day vocabulary.

A huge new wave of borrowing began in the middle of the twentieth century when regular and prolonged contact with large numbers of languages and cultures increased. Words for newly discovered flora and fauna, landscape features, clothing, foods and activities, as well as words associated with politics and institutions and new inventions have become part of the English lexicon. World trade, international politics and finance, travel and tourism, newspapers and television have all influenced the adoption of these words. Most English speaking people will have encountered words such as:

perestroika, glasnost, sputnik, fatwa, intifada, guerilla, as well as:

quiche, tacos, paella, crepe, kebab, cola.

It is not possible always to be certain precisely *when* particular words were adopted but we can be certain *where* they came from. Since the growth of dictionaries, we can obtain some idea of when a word became established from its first recorded entry in a dictionary. A small sample of words from across the world gives some sense of the variety.

France	cellar, anatomy, jewel, vogue, sculpture, café
Italy	fiasco, mafia, violin, giraffe, ciao
Germany	kindergarten, hamburger, lager, waltz
Holland/Belgium	easel, landscape, bluff, cruise, poppycock
Scandinavia	fiord, ski, ombudsman, tungsten, sauna, slalom
Spain	banana, mosquito, cork, hacienda, cannibal
Portugal	marmalade, cobra, albatross, molasses
Hungary	hussar, goulash
Croatia	cravat, slivovitz
Czech	pistol, robot, howitzer
Greece	anonymous, climax, tonic, mousaka, catastrophe
Turkey	coffee, kiosk, jackal, shish-kebab
Persia	bazaar, caravan, shah
North Africa	assassin, harem, sherbet, mohair, zero
Central Africa	safari, bongo, marimba
Southern Africa	gnu, impala, trek, apartheid, mamba
Russia	sputnik, samovar, borsch, agitprop, glasnost
North India	bungalow, chutney, dungarees, jungle, pyjamas, shampoo
South India	curry, catamaran, mulligatawny
Australia	kangaroo, boomerang, wombat, dingo
South America	puma, quinine, llama, poncho, coypu, jaguar
North America	chipmunk, skunk, totem, wigwam, toboggan, pecan
Caribbean	canoe, cannibal, barbecue, potato, yucca
Greenland/Iceland	geyser, mumps, saga, anorak, igloo

This is but a small sample of foreign borrowings – you will find hundreds more! Some of these words have arrived in the recent past, but many have been in our vocabulary for a very long time. All have unusual spellings which do not conform to common letter patterns in English, so care will be needed in checking these. An etymological dictionary should provide information about the sources of unusual words.

The other effect of British colonization was, of course, the spread of English. There are now varieties of English spoken and written throughout the world – English is now the dominant or official language in over 60 countries. These have variations in vocabulary, pronunciation and usage but remain English whether used in Australia, Africa, India and southern Asia, the Caribbean, Canada or America.

American English differs from British English in many ways which are now feeding back into the variety of English used in England – the wheel is turning full circle in this respect. Because there are close links between the two countries – historically, politically, economically and, especially, in entertainment – British English users, especially the young, frequently adopt 'Americanisms'. There are spelling differences which are significant. Many American spellings are simplified and apparently more rational than their English equivalents. British English often retains spellings which reflect the roots of words.

British	American
aeroplane	airplane
anaemia	anemia
archaeology	archeology
cauldron	caldron
cheque	check
councillor	councilor
doughnut	donut
jeweller	jeweler
marvellous	marvelous
plough	plow
programme (not computing)	program
traveller	traveler

American spelling tends to dispense with doubled letters, *ae-* and *-ough* forms. Children may encounter some American spellings in American-authored children's literature, though separate editions are often produced for the English and American markets – even the Dr Seuss books have English spelling in UK editions!

There are often stress differences in the pronunciation of words.

British	American
ad**dress**	**ad**dress
café	ca**fé**
garage	ga**rage**
maga**zine**	**mag**azine
week**end**	**week**end
mou**stache**	**mu**stache
prin**cess**	**prin**cess

And, of course, there are different words for some objects.

British	American
pocket money	allowance
rubbish	garbage/trash
bath	bathtub
petrol	gas(oline)
post code	zip code
holiday	vacation
postbox/pillarbox	mailbox
pavement	sidewalk
trainers	sneakers
(car) boot	trunk

Many people would like to stem the flow of Americanisms into British English, but it is inevitable that there will be accommodations and changes in the coming decades. More people are travelling in the USA and so will be familiar with American forms, and the influence of film and television on spoken forms is strong.

The English language is still absorbing elements of other languages as well as elements of other dialects and forms of English which have developed throughout the world. English has always been a sponge-like language, able to soak up what was needed from all the languages English-speaking people have encountered. It has never been and never will be static: it is a dynamic, living language and will go on changing and developing to meet new needs. Children studying the English language 50 or 100 years from now will probably discuss 'The changes which happened at the beginning of the 21st Century'!

The English language is in a constant state of change – most changes are very small and gradual. It is important for children to understand this, to investigate the history of English and to appreciate why modern English is as it is. Teachers need to provide starting points for investigations, especially of loaned words, which often fascinate children. There will be children in classes who will understand, speak and often be literate in one or more of the languages from which we have borrowed; they may be able to provide more vocabulary in that language. American English is now so much a part of children's lives that it is worthwhile looking at the differences between this and British English.

Why you need to know these facts

History and the English language

The NLS Framework for Teaching (1998) suggests investigation of borrowings from other languages in Year 5.

Teaching ideas

• Provide children with sets of loan words. Ask them to use etymological entries in dictionaries to locate the sources and languages from which the words come. When they have done this, invite them to think about how and why these words came into English. Discuss their ideas as a plenary activity.

• Give children some carefully selected loan words and ask them to use a world map or atlas to find the country the words came from. Look at where that source is in relation to the UK and discuss the possible ways in which the word reached us.

• Give children a set of common words written in American English spelling. Ask them to look up the words in an English dictionary and to 'correct' the American spelling. When several groups have done this, ask them to group the words according to the spelling differences.

> – American spelling has one *l*, English has two.
> – American spelling has *-or*, English has *–our*.
> – American spelling has *-e-*, English has *-ae-*.
> – American spelling has *-o* or *-ow*, English has *–ough*.

• Compile a class dictionary of translations from American words to English. Things to do with cars (automobiles) would be a good starting point:

British	American
boot	trunk
bonnet	hood
aerial	antenna
windscreen	windshield
numberplate	license plate
petrol gauge	gas gauge
gear lever	gear shift

Make sure the children notice the different spelling of *license*.

References and further reading

Crossley-Holland, K, illustrated by Keeping, C (1982)
Beowulf, Oxford: Oxford University Press
Harnett, C (1960) *A Load of Unicorn*, Harmondsworth:
Puffin Books

Useful resources for the history of English

Baugh, AC and Cable, T (1978) *A History of the English
Language*, (3rd edition), Englewood Cliffs: Prentice-Hall
Crystal, D (1987) *The Cambridge Encyclopedia of Language*,
Cambridge: Cambridge University Press
Crystal, D (1995) *The Cambridge Encyclopedia of The
English Language*, Cambridge: Cambridge University Press
Elmes, S (1999) *The Routes of English (1)*, London: BBC
Publications
Elmes, S (2000) *The Routes of English (2)*, London: BBC
Publications
Elmes, S (2000) *The Routes of English (3)*, London: BBC
Publications (all with CD-ROM of spoken extracts)
Flavell, L and R (1999) *The Chronology of Words and
Phrases – A Thousand Years in the History of English*,
Leicester: Silverdale Books
Flavell, L and R (1996) *Dictionary of Word Origins*, Kyle
Cathie Ltd
Fuller, S et al. (1990) *Language File*, London: Longman
Hoad, TF (ed)(1993) *The Concise Oxford Dictionary of
English Etymology*, Oxford: Oxford University Press
Matthews, CM (1979) *How Placenames Began*, London:
Beaver Books(Hamlyn)
McCrum,R et al. (1992 revised edition) *The Story of English*,
London: Faber and Faber/BBC Books
Mills, AD (ed) (1998) *Dictionary of English Place-names*,
Oxford: Oxford University Press
Richmond, J et al. (1982) *The Languages Book*, London:
English and Media Centre
Room, A (1999) *The Cassell Dictionary of Word Histories*,
London: Cassell

ICT resources

CD-ROM *Wordroot*, Wordroutes Ltd, Tel: 01767 600580

Chapter 5
Vocabulary development

A ll of the preceding chapters relate to vocabulary development in various ways. In this chapter the intention is to look at aspects of language study which can contribute very specifically to that development.

Looking at differences in dialect and the varieties of English used by speakers of the language has the potential to be both interesting and informative, as does looking at the way words change over time. In many areas of the country regional dialects are apparent in all social interactions outside school, so children need to be bi-dialectal if they are to be successful in the school context. Many children will also be using the languages of their communities. Though they may not be literate in these languages, they will probably be switching back and forth from the home language, to the language of their peer group, to Standard English (SE), and they will be very skilful in this. This linguistic achievement needs to be celebrated just as much as progress in learning SE forms in school. Similarly, in the context of looking at SE and dialect, children who use English as an additional language should have the opportunity to use and share that knowledge in the classroom.

An important strand in developing children's vocabulary is playing with words. Very young children relish language play of all kinds. We see this in playground rhymes, singing games and chants, tongue twisters and jokes. Many writers for children capitalise on this enjoyment and so can teachers. English is rich in idiomatic language – words and phrases which carry meanings beyond the actual words used – and investigation of the meanings and origins of some of these can be fascinating. Proverbs, too, reflect the history of both language and received wisdom.

A very specific range of terminology will be needed in discussing texts and the ways in which writers construct them. As children get older they need to understand the terminology used to talk about writers' use of figurative language; these terms also need to be added to children's vocabulary.

Vocabulary development is an important strand in the suggested framework for teaching for the literacy hour (1998) and teachers' own knowledge about some of the elements of this will need to be developed.

Standard English, dialect and slang

Subject facts

The acceptance of a particular dialect of English as the standard form began in the 15th century (see Chapter 4). The use of SE for written texts is now a substantial element of what children are taught in school. It is not suggested that teachers should attempt to change children's accents or even eliminate dialect forms in spoken English, but that children should be taught the forms, vocabulary and functions of SE and know when to use them. The intention should be to ensure clarity in communication in both speech and writing.

The National Curriculum (2000) Programme of Study requirement for teaching SE focuses on five 'most common non-standard usages in England':

- *subject–verb agreement* (they was)*;*
- *formation of past tense* (have fell, I done)*;*
- *formation of negatives* (ain't)*;*
- *formation of adverbs* (come quick)*;*
- *use of demonstrative pronouns* (them books).

All of these relate to grammatical structures rather than vocabulary and all are features of non-standard London English (or the much maligned Estuary English!). Other areas of the country would be likely to use other non-standard forms (for example, *yous two* (Liverpool) – *you two*; *I 've getten it* (Tyneside) – *I've got it*; *I ben't* (West Country) – *I'm not*). Concern about differences in vocabulary attract less attention.

Interesting work can be done with children using tape-recordings of people talking in different regional dialects. A starting point for some children might be the vocabulary of older residents in their own area.

Some children's literature offers opportunities for exploration of dialect forms. Inclusion of these texts will certainly lead to discussion about why the writer has chosen to use non-standard vocabulary and the meanings of words.

Princess Jazz and the Angels by Rachel Anderson is set in Glasgow and in the Punjab, with a mixed-race central character whose vocabulary is rich in Glaswegian dialect. Her vocabulary includes:
clarty (dirty)
wean (baby/child)
greetin' (crying)
deaving (wailing)
feart (frighten)
bide (stay)
couthy (friendly/snug)
stushie (commotion/rumpus)
sleekit (smooth)
blether (foolish chatter)

Other children's literature and writers offer the potential for looking at dialect, especially in dialogue (see 'Teaching ideas'). Looking at dialect words and their meanings can develop children's awareness of differences in language and why different regions have their own vocabularies.

In any work on SE and dialect, it is important to talk about 'difference' rather than 'correct'/'incorrect', 'right'/ 'wrong'. The aim is to *add* SE forms to the repertoire of those children who do not already use them and for them to understand when it is appropriate to use SE, not to tell them that the way they use English is *wrong*.

It is also important to be clear about the distinction between *dialect* and *accent*. SE is the dialectal variety of English which has the most prestige; it is the usual dialect of written English and its linguistic features are matters of grammar, vocabulary and orthography. SE is not a matter of pronunciation. SE can be spoken with any accent.

Accent is a matter of *pronunciation*; it is the way in which words are pronounced. Speakers can have a London accent, a Scots accent, a Devon accent, a Welsh accent, a Geordie accent, a Birmingham accent and still be using SE.

The accent considered by some to be the 'best' is *Received Pronunciation (RP)* which is the accent often used by those in powerful positions and is without any regional intonation. It is the accent taught to those learning English as a foreign language and is also the standard form used in linguistic research. RP was considered to be more widely understood than regional accents and was, therefore, adopted by the BBC when broadcasting began in the 1920s. Today RP is no longer associated with a social elite and the *BBC accent* is much changed from that which was heard fifty years ago. Many educated people now speak with an accent which is sometimes known as *modified RP* because it incorporates many features of the older RP accent alongside various regional characteristics. The most recent shift in this respect has been seen in the so-called *Estuary English* – the adoption of some characteristics of London speech into the accents of many educated people in the counties adjoining London, and beyond! Accents usually indicate where people come from but RP reveals only the speaker's social or educational background.

Slang

The *Oxford English Dictionary* defines *slang* as 'language of a highly colloquial type, considered as below the level of educated standard speech, and consisting either of new words or of current words employed in some special sense'. Many words or phrases which were once considered slang are now perfectly acceptable; words coined only twenty years ago are now part of ordinary vocabulary, for example, *snap* (photograph), *hair-do* (hair style), to *nip out* (to go out briefly), *smash hit* (successful performance in music), *twit* (foolish person), *cowboy* (unscrupulous operator), though they are still considered *colloquial.*

Colloquial English

This is informal, conversational idiom or vocabulary. A *colloquialism* is a word or phrase which would be appropriate in conversation or in an informal situation, but which would not be appropriate in writing.

> *'My dad's nutty about football.'* In this sentence *dad* and *nutty* would be described as colloquial, but not slang.
> *'I'll just nip out and take a snap of the children.'* In this sentence *nip out* and *snap* would be considered colloquial, but not slang.

Other words are still considered to be slang; some of these will gradually perhaps become acceptable but others will die out:

gob (mouth)
lugs (ears)
bum (bottom)
snotty (nasty/dirty)
grotty (unpleasant/useless)
snatch (robbery)
twocking (the act of breaking into a vehicle and driving away)
beak (judge/headmaster)
old bill (police)

Children know and use a whole range of slang vocabulary which they, sensibly, use only within their peer group. They generally know what is acceptable to a wider audience and what is unacceptable!

Many slang terms are used by those 'in the know' about a subject (for example, sailing, bird-watching, different sports, the law, acting, teaching) to show they are part of this group or club.

The language used to refer to shared ideas is often called *jargon*; most people within the group understand this but outsiders do not. Teachers are often guilty of using educational jargon when talking to others about schools, teaching and the curriculum; much of the jargon is made up of acronyms (see page 102).

Youth slang is another example of this – it excludes others and is a kind of code. Some words which were once part of this sub-culture are now so familiar they are no longer used by those who started them off and they sound rather dated, for example, *groovy, dodgy* (terms from the 1960s); *wicked, bad* (from the 1990s).

A word popular in 2000 was *pants* but the subsequent use of it as part of the Comic Relief campaign means it has moved beyond the youth culture in which it started!

The *neologism* (coining of a new word) stays new until people begin to use it without thinking, or it falls out of fashion and people stop using it altogether. Some remain in older texts but have been forgotten in everyday usage. Others have become part of ordinary usage, for example, *blurb* – which was coined by an American humorist, Gelett Burgess, in 1907. It now appears in dictionaries with a proper definition!

There is currently an increased emphasis on the use of SE in schools. Teachers need a very clear understanding of what SE is as well as knowledge about accent and dialect so that teaching about language can enable children to use SE forms in all appropriate contexts. A teacher's wide knowledge about the language forms in use will enable him or her to make work on SE really interesting for children.

Word meanings and vocabulary also change over time. Some words we might read in older texts do not now carry the same meanings that they originally had.

Word	Current meaning	Older meaning
vulgar	lacking in manners, taste; crude use of language	to do with ordinary people/the mass of the people
villain	wicked or malevolent person	workers on a country estate/ peasant (villein =old spelling)
silly	lacking in sense; absurd; superficial; feeble-minded	in 15th century meant *pitiable*; earlier meant blessed/happy
nice	pleasant/ kind/good	foolish/ ignorant/ delicate/shy
terrific	very good; very great or intense	extremely frightening
awful	nasty, unpleasant; ugly	overcome with awe; inspiring reverence or dread
presently	in a short while	immediately/ instantly
without	not having/lacking	outside

In the case of *wicked* (see above) the two meanings are held simultaneously, as follows:
wicked = very good/brilliant *and* morally bad, mischievous, unpleasant.

The process of change is very gradual. There are some who will always argue that the contemporary meanings are 'wrong' and that we should use the word with the meaning it formerly had!

Similarly, there are words which still exist with the same meaning, but are not in the active vocabulary of most younger people. These words are sometimes used by older people, for example, *gramophone, wireless, frock, permanent wave, gravy boat, sideboard.*

Teaching ideas

- Children's literature offers many opportunities for looking at the way SE and dialect forms vary.
Janet and Allan Ahlberg's *Burglar Bill* contains several examples in the speech of Burglar Bill and Burglar Betty of non-standard forms of English: 'Blow me down,' he says. 'It ain't no police cars, it's a baby!'

After reading the book, children could be asked what they noticed about this speech. They could be asked to change the non-standard forms into SE.

Other books which offer opportunities for this kind of work include:

> Anthony Browne *Walk in the Park* (some London non-standard)
> Jill Paton-Walsh *Thomas and the Tinners* (some Cornish dialect)
> Jill Paton-Walsh *Gaffer Samson's Luck* (East Anglian dialect and accent)
> Rachel Anderson *Princess Jazz & the Angels* (Glaswegian and some Irish dialect forms)
> Berlie Doherty *Children of Winter* (Derbyshire dialect of 17th century characters)
> John Agard *Go Noah, Go!* (Caribbean English)

- If your school is in an area where dialect forms are prevalent in everyday speech, arrange for children to interview older residents (perhaps about their memories of school) and tape-record the conversations. Listen to these and identify non-standard vocabulary forms. Compile a local dialect dictionary.

If you have friends in other parts of the country, ask them to do the same and swap tapes. Listening to unfamiliar dialects is both fascinating and challenging for children. Alternatively, use some of the recordings which are commercially available.

- Compile a class Slang Dictionary and investigate the origins of some of the slang/jargon.

Playing with language

The desire to explore the potential and limits of the language is deeply embedded in children and adults alike. Some writers for children are extremely skilful in this respect and their work can be invaluable in exploring words with children. At a very early age children are able to play with both the sounds of the language and word meanings.

Subject facts

Rhyme

The use of rhyme in language play is the foundation of nursery rhymes and volumes of verse and poetry for children. Rhyme patterns are quickly perceived by very young children and become a source of entertainment even in nonsense chants made up by them. In this rhyme, which was tape-recorded when Simon was five-and-a-half, he is simply playing with the sounds and enjoying saying them, but clearly understands what rhyme is all about:

> *Once upon a ping-pong,*
> *There was a little jing-jong,*
> *Sitting on a ding-dong,*
> *Eating up his fing-fong.*
> *He was a bong-bong.*

Rhyme can be defined as words which have the same sound in the final syllable. Crystal (1995) defines it as 'a correspondence of syllables, especially at the end of poetic lines'.

Rhymes can be of different kinds, as the following example demonstrates.

One, **two**,	Eleven, **twelve**,
Buckle my **shoe**;	Dig and **delve**;
Three, **four**,	Thirteen, <u>fourteen</u>,
Knock at the **door**;	Maids a-<u>courting</u>;
Five, **six**,	Fifteen, <u>sixteen</u>,
Pick up **sticks**;	Maids in the <u>kitchen</u>;
Seven, **eight**,	Seventeen, <u>eighteen</u>,
Lay them **straight**	Maids a-<u>waiting</u>;
Nine, **ten**	Nineteen, **twenty**,
A big fat **hen**;	My plate's **empty**.

Vocabulary development

In this nursery rhyme, the words in bold, in pairs, are *full rhymes* – that is, the vowel phonemes/sounds of the pairs of words are the same. The underlined words in the second half of the verse have vowel phonemes or sounds which are similar, but not the same; these are *half rhymes*.

Sometimes, *internal rhyme* is used. In this, a word at the end of a line is rhymed with a word earlier in the line, or words within a line are rhymed. This is done, with great comic effect in the verse *Pass the Jam, Jim* by Kaye Umansky.

> Hurry, **Mabel**, lay that **table**!   (internal rhyme)
> **Jane**, put **Wayne** back in his <u>pram</u>!   (internal rhymes)
> Where's the **bread, Fred**?   (internal rhyme)
> **Bread** I **said, Fred**.   (internal rhymes)
> Pass the jam, Jim,
> Jam, Jim, <u>jam</u>.

The conventional full rhyme, at the ends of lines, occurs only with the underlined words, *pram/jam*. The remainder of the verse continues in the same vein!

Alliteration

Alliteration occurs when adjacent words in a phrase start with the same phoneme. It is a device used by writers of prose and poetry to create a particular effect. In the example *'smooth snakes slither silently in the long grass'* the repeated /s/ sound suggests the movement of the snake. This repeated /s/ sound appears at the end of the word *grass* and is an example of consonance. When the repeated sound appears elsewhere in a word, rather than in the initial position, the device is called *consonance*.

Alliteration is one aspect of language play which children can appreciate as they become phonologically aware. Playing with words with the same initial sound is an enjoyable activity for them. Such games range from making up phrases to attach to people's names (for example, *Happy, helpful Hanife; Big, brave Ben; Clever, climbing Carly*) to longer tongue twisters:

> Hamida had a happy hippopotamus in her house.
> Sleepy Simone sat sewing simple stitches.
> Ben bakes beautiful big buns.

Whole nonsense stories can be constructed from words beginning with the same letter:

> Tony the tyrannosaurus tripped over Tommy the tiger, tossed Tracey the turtle into the teapot, then trod on the television in the tent. He trod on the toad's toes, tickled the turtle's tummy and tricked Timmy the tortoise into taking the trumpet from the tricerotops.

This was composed by a group of Year 4 children.

The writer Margaret Atwood, whose work is not generally associated with humorous writing for children, has created a whole picture book in this manner, *Princess Prunella and the Purple Peanut*, and has clearly thoroughly enjoyed herself doing so!

Princess Prunella was proud, prissy and pretty and unhappily very spoiled. She would never pick up her playthings, plump her pillows, or put away her pens, pencils and puzzles. Instead, after her breakfast of prunes and porridge, and her pineapple and passion-fruit punch, presented in a copper cup painted with porpoises and spiders, she would parade around all day, in puffy petticoats sprinkled with sparkling pink sequins...

Assonance

When the sound repeated is a phoneme within words, the term used to describe the effect is *assonance*. Poets use this device to create atmosphere. An example is the title of the poem 'Anthem for Doomed Youth', where Wilfred Owen creates an ominous, doleful sense of what is to come in the poem itself.

In Ted Hughes' poem 'Gulls', we see both alliteration and assonance, as well as rhyme, work superbly to create a sense of the wind and air movement through which the gulls battle.

Gulls
Gulls are glanced from the lift
Of cliffing air
And left
Loitering in the descending drift,
Or tilt gradient and go
Down steep, invisible clefts in the grain
Of air, blading against the blow

Onomatopoeia

Closely allied to alliteration and assonance is *onomatopoeia*, where words are used to recreate a particular noise. The words used to describe animal sounds for young children are simple examples of this:

> moo (cows)
> baa (sheep)
> woof (dog)
> miaow (cat)
> quack (duck)

Onomatopoeia is used often to replicate the noise of movements or explosions:

> boom, crash, whoosh, clatter, buzz, bleep, hiss, gurgle, clip-clop, zoom, rat-at-tat, hush

Cartoonists make great use of this device by making up words to communicate the sounds in comic strips:

> ker-plonk, pow, phsst, splurge, whump, hee-hee, yowch

Perhaps inspired by these, children will often make up their own onomatopoeic words to express the sounds of machinery:

> nee-naa, nee-naa (fire-engine), boing, boing (something bouncing)

Making up words

The English language has a variety of words which are amalgamations of existing words. These have been coined to express new concepts and are known as *lexical blends* or *portmanteau* words. This latter term was invented by Lewis Carroll but has since gained some linguistic respectability. As the name suggests it means words packed with more than one meaning – a portmanteau is a large suitcase which opens into two parts (portmanteau is a French word meaning, literally, 'carry mantle/coat').

> motel (motoring hotel)
> Oxbridge (Oxford/Cambridge)
> brunch (meal that is neither breakfast nor lunch but in between)
> docudrama (part documentary, part fictional drama)
> heliport (helicopter airport)
> smog (smoke and fog)
> breathalyser (breath analyser)
> readathon (reading marathon)

These lexical blends amalgamate two ideas.

Diminutives

A variation on this, combining the idea of smallness with an existing noun, is the *diminutive*. These are commonly made in English by adding suffixes:

> -kin   as in lambkin, Peterkin
> -let   as in starlet, piglet, booklet
> -ette   as in maisonnette, majorette, cigarette

These are accepted as normal words, but one of these suffixes is sometimes added to a noun in a humorous or playful way within a family or group to indicate a little something, for example, *pusskin* (little cat), *mummykins* (little Mummy).

Many writers for children are masters and mistresses of linguistic invention and their work is much appreciated by their young readers. The classic examples are to be found in Lewis Carroll, of course.

Jabberwocky
> *Twas brillig, and the slithy toves*
> *Did gyre and gimble in the wabe;*
> *All mimsy were the borogoves,*
> *And the mome raths outgrabe.*

Roald Dahl produced books in which a whole new invented vocabulary is used with great comic effect. It is rare for child readers to have difficulty understanding this. In *The BFG* the names of the bad giants express their activities graphically: *Bonecruncher, Fleshlumpeater, Childchewer, Gizzardgulper.* The BFG's language is a delight:

> *'How wondercrump'* cried the BFG, still beaming. *'How whoopsey-splunkers! How absolutely squiffling! I is all of a stutter.'*

(page 57)

Although these words do not exist outside this book, their meaning is very apparent!

In *Esio Trot* and in *The Vicar of Nibbleswick* Dahl's invented vocabulary is simply reversed words, for example, *Esio Trot* is *tortoise; teg reggib* is *get bigger; tup no taf* is *put on fat; emoc no* is *come on*! The Vicar's problem is a condition which causes him to reverse many words, with extremely comic (and often cheeky) effect. *God* becomes *dog,* sip becomes *pis, trespasses* becomes *sessapsert, knits* becomes *stink.*

What Dahl is doing in these books is closely allied to palindromes, which are another aspect of language play.

Palindromes

These are words or phrases which are the same when read or spelled from left to right or right to left.

> eve
> pup
> level
> madam   Madam, I'm Adam!
> able was I ere I saw Elba (Napoleon!)

This is not a serious literary device but children often do enjoy exploring the possibilities for palindromic words and it is a term they enjoy knowing! Looking for palindromes can be a way of getting them to look closely at the letters in words.

A much more serious kind of word play involves the creation of new vocabulary in imaginary contexts. We see this at an adult level in the creation of Newspeak in Orwell's *1984*. Writers of fantasy for children also frequently invent new vocabulary to express novel concepts and ideas. Philip Pullman, for example, invents some glorious names for fireworks and their ingredients in *The Firework Maker's Daughter*: *shimmering coins, Golden Sneezes, Crackle Dragons,* made of *thunder-grains, cloud-powder, salts-of-shadow, glimmer-juice* and much more!

In the fantasy worlds Pullman creates in the *Northern*

Lights trilogy, artefacts, creatures, people and places all have inventive names which draw on real linguistic roots to express new ideas. Lyra is the keeper of an instrument called an *alethiometer* which tells her the truth; the word is created from the Greek *aletheia* meaning *truth* and *metron* meaning a measuring instrument. The word *alethic* exists in English and relates to a branch of philosophy and logic which deals with the concepts of truth, necessity, possibility and contingency – precisely the qualities revealed by the *alethiometer.* The layers of meaning embedded in the invented vocabulary of writers like Pullman are rich sources of nourishment for young readers.

Why you need to know these facts

Literature for children makes use of all of these ways of playing with language and children need to understand the vocabulary used to talk about these devices. The National Curriculum and the NLS includes this terminology in the teaching suggested for the whole primary range, so teachers need to be clear themselves about the terms.

Teaching ideas

• Select poems with clear rhyming patterns and ask children to identify the words which rhyme. With these as a starting point, ask a group to take one or two rhymes each and then to collect more words which have the same rhyme. A development of this could be to look at how the vowel phonemes are represented with different vowels, digraphs and trigraphs and then to group the words according to the spellings.

• Playing with alliteration can begin at a very early age. Make up alliterative descriptions for each member of the class and make a class book of these. The same can be done with foods or animals:

terrible tigers	bendy bananas
beautiful bears	crispy cakes
clever cats	dangerous doughnuts
dancing dogs	sizzling sausages

• With older children show some of the alphabet books which use alliteration in this way (for example, *Animalia* – Graeme Base; *A Beastly Collection* – Jonathon Coudrille (this is now out of print, but libraries may have copies);

Comic and Curious Cats – Martin Leman). Invite the children to make up their own alliterative sentences about people or animals. Once they have done some of this, move on to the creation of whole stories which are alliterative. This can be a very productive group activity, especially if the results are made into class books. Margaret Atwood's book is a helpful model for this.

• When working with poems, look for examples of assonance; talk about the effect created and then invite children to write themselves using assonance. The work of Ted Hughes, both poetry and prose, is often rich in assonance. For older children, carefully chosen poems by Tennyson or Browning or Alfred Noyes (*The Highwayman*) could be used. Show children how alliteration, assonance and rhyme work together.

• Select a poem or a short prose extract which has an interesting rhyme scheme, examples of alliteration and assonance or examples of onomatopoeia. When children are very familiar with the piece, ask them to identify the devices the writer has used. This is best done as a paired or group activity so that children can discuss their ideas.

• Invite children to bring comic strips (especially Beano annuals, Superman, Spiderman, Batman) into the classroom and use these to show onomatopoeia at work. Let children make up their own comic-strip stories using this device.

• Using *The Firework Maker's Daughter* as a starting point, ask children to invent even more new words for ingredients and fireworks. If this is successful, look at the names advertisers devise for new products and do the same for new drinks or confectionery. Devising slogans for their invented products could also draw on children's knowledge of how onomatopoeia works.

• Look at some of the common lexical blends and ask children to make up some of their own. Themes could range from things done in school to holidays, travelling or sports. Give some examples, for example *literagroup* – a group for literacy hour activities; *numaplen* – a plenary session in numeracy; *hushathon* – a sponsored silence marathon. A similar game could be played adding one of the diminutive suffixes: *storylet* – a very short story; *roomette* – a very small room; *tunelet* – a short tune; *cakelet* – a small cake; *boxette* – a little box.

• Talk about palindromes; teach children the term and make a class collection.

Texts, imagery and figurative language

Teachers' work with children requires a knowledge, not just about different kinds of text, but also about the literary devices writers use in creating their texts.

Genre
The term *genre* has been much used in recent years in discussion about the kinds of text which children read and write and the structure of those texts.

The word genre used simply to be applied to varieties of literary or fiction texts; stories are 'in the fairy-tale genre' or the 'science-fiction genre'. Each genre has specific characteristics, including story elements, patterns of language and vocabulary. For example, a story beginning 'Once upon a time...' is likely to be a fairy story.

The term also relates to reader interest and the way publishers and teachers indicate what kind of book or story something is, for the benefit of potential readers – for example, Romance, Science Fiction, Horror, Adventure.

We now use the term to talk about texts more widely. The National Curriculum and the National Literacy Strategy require teachers and children to have a sound understanding of the purpose, the characteristics and the structures of many kinds of text, both fiction and non-fiction. Each of these text types is called a *genre*.

Fiction and literary genres
These would include myth, legend, fairy story, traditional or folk stories, fable, science fiction, historical fiction, mystery, adventure, fantasy, thriller, ghost story, realistic fiction, stories from other cultures and traditions, as well as poetry and playscripts.

The NC range is wide but does not subdivide the variety of genres for reading as much as this. Children must write narrative, poetry and playscripts.

Non-fiction and non-literary genres
The NC includes diaries, autobiography, biography, letters, newspapers, magazines, reference material and ICT texts in the range for reading.

Children must learn to write in the main genres of narrative, recount, report, procedure and instruction, explanation, persuasion, discussion and argument. In addition to understanding the structure and organisation of these genres, children must be able to make use of specialist vocabulary and words associated with a particular kind of writing.

This section will not address issues to do with the structure of any of these genres, but will focus on the kinds of *imagery* and *figurative language* associated with literary texts. The strategies and devices considered here are most generally associated with poetic writing. It is true that writers of poetry make use of all of these, but writers of prose often do so, too.

It is also important to remember that writing can be both affective and powerful without the use of these devices. Children should not be made to feel that 'good' writing is full of imagery, metaphor, simile and personification and that writing lacking such devices is poorer.

Imagery

Imagery is 'the use of language to create a vivid sensory image' (NLS, 1998). The writing conveys ideas or feelings through the image presented. The image is usually visual but can also appeal to other senses. In the following poem Robert Louis Stevenson describes the feelings of a child climbing the stairs to bed in the days before electricity – the child's only light is a flickering candle. His fear is conveyed convincingly through the creation of strong visual images.

Shadow March
  All round the house is the jet-black night;
  It stares through the window-pane;
  It crawls in the corners, hiding from the light,
  And it moves with the moving flame.

  Now my little heart goes a-beating like a drum,
  With the breath of the Bogie in my hair;
  And all round the candle the crooked shadows come
  And go marching along up the stair.

  The shadow of the balusters, the shadow of the lamp,
  The shadow of the child that goes to bed –
  All the wicked shadows coming tramp, tramp, tramp,
  With the black light overhead.

The visual images of darkness and flickering light are the

strongest, but there are also elements of the auditory (the beating heart and the tramping shadows) and the tactile (the movement of the hair). The child's feelings are communicated powerfully to the reader.

Stevenson creates these images in several ways. He begins by personifying the night which 'stares, crawls, hid(es) from the light' and moves, as a person would. This device is called *personification* – the attribution of human characteristics to 'non-human agents or objects or abstract concepts' (NLS, 1998). Stevenson uses personification again later in the poem, for the shadows which are 'crooked' and 'wicked' and 'go marching along up the stair' with a 'tramp, tramp, tramp', and for 'the Bogie' whose 'breath' the child can feel.

Personification is a type of *metaphor,* which is where a 'writer writes about something as if it were really something else' (NLS, 1998). In Stevenson's poem, night and the shadows are endowed with intentions; in their crawling, hiding, staring, marching and tramping, they seem to the child to intend to harm him – they are a threat.

Some prose writers make use of metaphor in similar ways. The work of Kevin Crossley-Holland, for example, is rich in metaphor (good examples can be found in his short story, *Storm).*

Writers sometimes make direct comparisons of things, in order to convey the qualities of something they are writing about. These are called *similes* – when 'the writer creates an image in readers' minds by comparing a subject to something else' (NLS, 1998). In the Stevenson poem, the child compares the beating of his heart to the beating of a drum – 'Now my little heart goes a-beating like a drum'.

Similes are commonly used in English, not just in literary writing but also in everyday speech and writing, and they are often idiomatic (see page 159). They are generally recognised by the use of *like* or *as* in the comparison, as shown in the following example:

His face was as green as grass.
The children were as quiet as mice/as good as gold.
She was as old as the hills.
The choir sang like angels.
The angry cat was like a tiger.
He rushed through the house like a whirlwind.
The bluebells were like a carpet under the trees.

Similes are used so generally that often we hardly notice

them. In literary writing, whether poetry or prose, writers capture our attention by creating fresh images in their use of simile.

Figurative language

All of these literary devices are used in the creation of *figurative language*. Figurative language is when writers make use of simile, metaphor, personification 'to create a particular impression or mood' (NLS, 1998). It uses more complex structures and vocabulary than is used in everyday speech or writing to create a 'poetic' effect. The distinction between the literary language of writers of poetry and prose and everyday language is one which children perceive in their reading. They understand the differences between 'book language' and ordinary language very early on, but developing explicit knowledge about how texts are constructed comes much later when they are fluent readers, able to reflect on the devices writers use.

Why you need to know these facts

Most teachers will have done some work on literary texts as part of their own education, but the terminology required to discuss texts may well have been forgotten. The requirements of the NC and the NLS mean that teachers must be able to draw confidently on the vocabulary needed to teach about the literature encountered in the classroom.

Although this language is not used in the early stages of primary English, it is a part of children's work in KS2. The children's own vocabulary must be developed to encompass this terminology.

Teaching ideas

● Children need to have had considerable experience of hearing and reading poetry before they are able to reflect on how writers use figurative language. They need to hear the rhythms and cadences of both classic and modern poetry.

There are now versions of some older poems available in well-illustrated editions for children. Some good examples are, Charles Keeping – *The Highwayman, The Lady of Shallot*; Michael Foreman – *A Child's Garden of Verses*; Andre Amstutz – *The Pied Piper of Hamelin*. Reading poetry aloud to children should be one of the first teaching strategies.

● Ask children to collect similes from their own reading as well as those they hear in people's speech. This device is

used very frequently so the collection should grow fast.
Once there are sufficient in the class collection, select some
of the most vivid comparisons, look at the images they
create and talk about why they are effective.

- Select poems from collections of modern poets which are
written in contrasting styles, for example, Charles Causley,
Ted Hughes, John Mole, Michael Rosen, Roger McGough,
Kit Wright, John Foster, John Agard, Grace Nichols, Gareth
Owen, Judith Nicholls, Gillian Clark. Some modern writers
use little figurative language and others use a good deal –
both styles can communicate very effectively with readers.
An analysis and comparison of two poems by writers whose
styles are very different can be most revealing.

- Once children are familiar with a range of poetry, ask
them to write some themselves. Show them some poetry
written by other children (there are now published
collections from competitions and the *Times Educational
Supplement* publishes one most weeks) so that they can see
that children can write very successfully. Choose topics or
themes which children are likely to have feelings or views
about.

- Choose a poem or an extract from a longer piece of prose
writing which contains examples of:
    – similes
    – metaphors, including personification
    – integration of sound features (assonance, alliteration,
    onomatopoeia, rhyme) into metaphors and similes.
Once children are familiar with the writing, ask them to
discuss the language and to identify the ways in which the
writer creates images.

Idiomatic English

Subject facts

The English language is particularly rich in idioms and a
knowledge of these is necessary for someone to be a truly
fluent user of the language. An *idiom* can be defined as 'a
combination of words with a special meaning that cannot
be inferred from its parts' (Gulland and Hinds-Howell,
1986). The NLS (1998) says an idiom is 'a phrase often used
by a group of people which is not meant literally. Its
meaning is understood by the people who use it, but cannot
be inferred from the individual words.' This definition

suggests that the meaning of a particular idiom may be understood only by 'a group of people'. In fact, the range of idioms in general use and understood by the majority of English speakers is extremely wide.

There are different types of idiom.

1. Some are made up of words which do have a literal meaning, but do not make much sense unless you know the metaphorical meaning – the idiom.

> He let the cat out of the bag.

This could mean, literally, that a cat was released from a bag. Though why the cat was in the bag and needed to be released is unclear: why would anyone put a cat in a bag? The metaphor of freeing the cat is used to indicate that someone has given away information which was supposed to be secret (that is, locked 'in the bag'). This is the idiomatic meaning.

> Jill wouldn't say boo to a goose.

This could mean, literally, that Jill was unwilling to approach a goose and say 'Boo'. It would be perfectly possible to do this, but why would anyone want to? A goose, which was often used as a guard, might make a fuss, but would be easily scared off, so there could be a historical reason for the phrase. The metaphor of someone unwilling to scare off or shout (mildly) at a goose is used to indicate that the subject is so timid that they would be unlikely to make even the mildest of protests. This is the idiomatic meaning.

2. Other idioms have no literal meaning at all, only an idiomatic one:

> Shall we go Dutch?

This has only the idiomatic meaning of 'Shall we both pay for our own parts?' There may have been something in the past which suggested that Dutch people would do this, to suggest the idiom in the first place.

> That place has gone to pot.

This has only the idiomatic meaning of the place having deteriorated. It is difficult to imagine where it came from.

3. There are a number of idioms which compare someone's behaviour to that of an animal or another person. In one sense they are similes.

> She was like a bull in a china shop.

Literally this means that she was behaving as a bull would; if a bull (for whatever reason!) were to find himself in a china shop he would be likely to rush around impetuously smashing the china. Again the bull is metaphorical, its typical behaviour is compared to the person who is destructive, thoughtless and clumsy. This is the idiomatic meaning.

> Pete was like a dog with two tails, when he won the prize.

Literally this means that Pete was behaving as a happy dog would do. Dogs wag their tails when they are pleased; if they were exceptionally pleased they would like to have double the amount of tail to wag and sometimes wag so much that they may look as if they have two tails! The comparison here with the behaviour of a very happy dog conveys the fact that Pete is exceptionally happy and very pleased with himself!

Some idioms began as quotations from literary writing. Perhaps the most influential writer in this respect has been Shakespeare. Many phrases were introduced by Shakespeare and have since become part of idiomatic English. Some of these now have meanings slightly different from Shakespeare's but all are in use in modern English.

Phrase/Meaning	Source
What the dickens! This is a euphemism for *what the devil* = what on earth/whatever	*Merry Wives of Windsor*
hoist with his own petard A petard was a small bomb which sometimes exploded in firing, blowing up the military engineer = to be caught in a trap intended for someone else	*Hamlet*
salad days 'when I was green in judgement' = inexperienced youth	*Antony & Cleopatra*
a tower of strength = a person who gives support, comfort etc.	*Richard III*
beggars all description used originally of Cleopatra = to be so remarkable that no one can describe it – now used in sense of appalling.	*Antony & Cleopatra*
it's Greek to me I cannot understand a word/it's like a foreign language.	*Julius Caesar*
to play fast and loose to behave in an insincere and unreliable manner	*Antony & Cleopatra*
cold comfort of little or no comfort	*King John*

There are many more such phrases from Shakespeare's work which have become part of the English idiom.

There are idioms drawn from a vast range of topics, including from animals of all kinds, plants, foodstuffs, the body, the full range of colours, numbers, occupations and clothing. Any one of these topics could be taken as a theme for investigation of idioms.

Clichés

Some of the most frequently used idioms are considered to
be *clichés*. These are words or expressions which have lost
much of their force through over-exposure; they are
considered to be hackneyed and trite. Not all phrases which
are considered to be clichés are idioms; some are simply
over-used phrases.

Her eyes shone like stars	At the end of the day
He has given up the ghost	To put it in a nutshell
The baby was as good as gold	To beat about the bush
She was as pretty as a picture	As large as life
I have left no stone unturned	Every Tom, Dick and Harry
To make a mountain out of a molehill	On your own head be it
To add insult to injury	Be that as it may
It takes all sorts	In this day and age
You can't keep a good man down	It will end in tears

Whether or not a phrase is considered a cliché is very
much a matter of opinion and style. Some books of usage
list phrases described as 'useful idiomatic phrases' which
in other books are given as clichés!

When children first discover phrases like these, they can
become entranced by them and pepper their writing with
them. If they are used judiciously they can be very effective
and children will certainly enjoy experimenting with them,
though they should probably be discouraged from using
phrases which, to the adult ear, are simply deemed to be
clichés.

Proverbs

A *proverb* is a particular kind of idiomatic expression.
Proverbs are short, pithy phrases or sentences which
express some kind of commonly held belief or traditional
wisdom. The proverb is a way of passing this wisdom on to
future generations.

Proverbs are brief, have vivid images and often make use
of rhythm, rhyme or alliteration so that they are easily
memorable. The origins of proverbs are usually not known
but children can enjoy hypothesising about how they arose
because the images created are often fairly clear.

There are some typical proverbs in the example which
follows:

Vocabulary development

Proverb	Meaning
Let sleeping dogs lie be!	Don't make trouble; leave it be!
Don't put all your eggs in one basket	Don't rely on just one thing, then you won't lose everything if it lets you down
Once bitten, twice shy	If something has hurt or upset you once, you won't take a similar risk again
It's no use crying over spilt milk	There's no point in getting upset over mistakes you can't undo
All that glitters is not gold	Appearances can be deceptive; something may not be what it seems

Why you need to know these facts

The vocabulary of English is full of these idiomatic phrases, some of which we all understand without much effort and others which seem strange and even archaic. Children's reading and study of literature will uncover some and investigation of their meanings can be worthwhile. Work on idioms appears in the NLS Framework for Teaching from Year 5 when it is suggested that children be asked to investigate some common idioms and clichés and to consider the use of these in their own writing.

Amazing facts

A surprisingly large number of idioms have been taken as titles by writers, musicians and film makers.

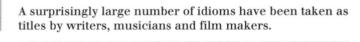

Cold Comfort Farm
All our Yesterdays
Salad Days
To the Manner (Manor) Born

Love is Blind
Free as Air
Roman Holiday
The Darling Buds of May

There are certainly many more. It would be interesting to compile your own list!

Be aware that children for whom English is an additional language may have difficulty understanding beyond the literal meaning of an idiom. Even children who are apparently fluent users of English may be confused by some idioms.

1. Collect idioms from people's speech. Write these down and discuss the meanings.
2. Collect idiomatic phrases from written texts. Look at the meanings and try to find alternative ways of expressing the same ideas.

Use the class collections of idioms to discuss whether they are clichés or 'useful phrases'. Make two lists.

Take one of the topics for which there are many idiomatic phrases (for example, colours, foods, parts of the body) and think of or look for as many as can be found.

Red	Blue
a red rag to a bull	to feel blue
paint the town red	once in a blue moon
see red	a blue-eyed boy
red tape	out of the blue
caught red-handed	a blue-stocking
a red letter day	blue-blooded
to be in the red	make the air turn blue

Look these up in a Dictionary of Idioms (some will be listed in some standard dictionaries) and find out the meaning and, where possible the origin of the idiom.

Collect idioms which can be illustrated and ask children to illustrate the literal meaning and then to write an explanation of the idiomatic meaning. These phrases lend themselves well to this activity, but there many more:

raining cats and dogs	as though he had been pulled through a hedge backwards
a bull in a china shop	taking the bull by the horns
over the moon	pulling the wool over his eyes
putting the cat amongst the pigeons	letting the cat out of the bag

• Make a class collection or book of proverbs. Illustrate the literal meaning and write an explanation of the advice being offered.

Resources

References and further reading

Ahlberg, J and A (1977) *Burglar Bill,* London: Heinemann
Anderson, R (1994) *Princess Jazz and the Angels,* London: Heinemann
Atwood, M (1995) *Princess Prunella and the Purple Peanut,* Bristol: Barefoot Books
Base, G (1986) *Animalia,* Harmondsworth: Penguin Books Ltd
Crystal, D (1995) *The Cambridge Encyclopedia of the English Language,* Cambridge: Cambridge University Press
Crossley-Holland, K (1985) *Storm,* London: Heinemann Educational (Banana Books)
Dahl, R (1982) *The BFG,* London: Jonathan Cape
Dahl, R (1990) *Esio Trot,* London: Jonathan Cape
Dahl, R (1992) *The Vicar of Nibbleswicke*, Harmondsworth: Penguin Books Ltd
Gulland, D and Hinds-Howell, D (1986) *The Penguin Dictionary of English Idioms*, Harmondsworth: Penguin Books
Hughes, T (1999) 'Gulls' in *The Mermaid's Purse*, London: Faber and Faber
National Literacy Strategy Framework for Teaching (1998), London: DfEE
Pullman, P (1995) *The Firework Maker's Daughter*, London: Transworld Publishers
Pullman, P (1995) *Northern Lights,* London: Scholastic Children's Books
Stevenson, Robert Louis (1996 – first published 1885) *A Child's Garden of Verses,* London: Gollancz
Umansky, K (1993) *Pass the Jam, Jim,* London: Random House (Red Fox)

1. For language study (dialect)

Agard, J (1990) *Go Noah, Go!,* London: Hodder and Stoughton
Anderson, R (1994) *Princess Jazz & the Angels*, London: Heinemann
Browne, A (1977) *Walk in the Park,* London: Hamish Hamilton

Doherty, B (1985) *Children of Winter*, London: Methuen
Paton-Walsh, J (1995) *Thomas and the Tinners*, London:
Macdonald Young Books
Paton-Walsh, J (1984) *Gaffer Samson's Luck*,
Harmondsworth: Penguin Books
Elmes, S (1999) *The Routes of English (1)*, London: BBC
Publications
Elmes, S (2000) *The Routes of English (2)*, London: BBC
Publications
Elmes, S (2000) *The Routes of English (3)*, London: BBC
Publications (all with CD-ROM of spoken extracts)

2. For work on idioms and proverbs

Flavell, L and R (1994) *Dictionary of Idioms and their
Origins*, London: Kyle Cathie Ltd
Flavell, L and R (1994) *Dictionary of Proverbs and their
Origins*, London: Kyle Cathie Ltd
Gulland, D and Hinds-Howell, D (1986) *The Penguin
Dictionary of English Idioms*, Harmondsworth: Penguin
Books
Hughes, S (1980) *Over the Moon. A Book of Sayings*, London:
Faber and Faber
Hughes, S (1979) *Make Hay While the Sun Shines. A Book of
Proverbs*, London: Faber and Faber

Spelling and vocabulary
Appendix

William Caxton

Caxton was born in Kent. As he writes in the prologue to the first English printed book, *The Recuyell of the Historyes of Troy*:

> *I was born and lerned myn Englissh in Kente in the*
> *Weeld, where I doubte not is spoken as brode and rude*
> *Englissh as in ony place in England*

The exact date of Caxton's birth is not known but by 1438 he was apprenticed to a London mercer (textile dealer), which suggests a birth date somewhere between 1415 and 1424. He went to Bruges in the early 1440s where he prospered as a mercer and became governor of the English trading company, the Merchant Venturers in 1462.

In 1471 he travelled to Cologne and remained there for 18 months learning about printing. Armed with this new knowledge, he collaborated with a Flemish calligrapher, Colard Mansion, and set up a printing press in Bruges. This press produced the first book printed in English in late 1473 or early 1474. *The Recuyell of the Historyes of Troy* had been translated from the French by Caxton himself. He was much indebted to Margaret, Duchess of Burgundy, for her help in this because, as he admits in the prologue, he had never been in France and his French was 'unperfect'!

Caxton returned to England in 1476 to set up his wooden printing press in a shop within the precincts of Westminster Abbey, to be close to the court. The shop was called The Red Pale; unfortunately, the significance of this sign is not known. The first book printed here was *The Dictes* or *Sayengis of the Philosophres* in 1477, which was translated from the French by Lord Rivers. In Westminster, Caxton published over 80 items, some in more than one edition. Many of these were his own translations and included prologues and epilogues in which Caxton told much about his aims as a publisher. He published the popular courtly tales in both verse and prose, including Chaucer's *Canterbury Tales* and a translation of Malory's *Morte d'Arthur*, as well as a variety of ordinary texts, such as phrase books, a Latin grammar, devotional pieces and statutes.

Little is known about how Caxton worked – how many presses there were or whether he worked on more than one book at a time. We do know that some books were produced very rapidly whilst others took much longer.

When Caxton died in 1491, his business was taken over by Wynkyn de Worde, his assistant, who moved the press in 1500 from Westminster to Fleet Street.

Richard Mulcaster

Mulcaster was born around 1530 and died in 1611. He became the Headmaster of the Merchant Taylor's School in London. He wrote several books on education and was a committed advocate for the use of English, rather than Latin, in scholarship. At this time there were fierce arguments all over Europe, with one side advocating the retention of Latin for writing scholarly works because the vernacular (English, in England) was 'crude, limited and immature, fit for popular literature, but little else'. Those on the other side, including Mulcaster, argued for English. Mulcaster wrote:

> *I do not think that anie language, be it whatsoever, is better able to utter all arguments, either with more pith, or greater planess, than our English tung is*

Mulcaster was also a great advocate for the regularisation of English spelling. In 1582 he produced his Elementarie, which provided recommended spellings for nearly 9000 words and had a great influence on grammarians and pronunciation teachers. He argued that:

> *It were a thing verie praiseworthie in my opinion... if someone well learned... would gather all the words which we use in our English tung... into one dictionarie.*

It was also Mulcaster who first suggested the addition of an *e* at the end of words of one syllable, with a long vowel sound, to indicate pronunciation, for example *take, save, hide* – what we now know as the silent *e*, or *the split digraph.* He thought that children would be able to distinguish these words more easily in their reading if the *e* were added. Although the suggestion was widely adopted, printers often added an *e* to words which did not have a long vowel sound, giving us a crop of exceptions, for example *give, love.*

Samuel Johnson

Johnson was born in 1709 in Lichfield in Staffordshire. He was the son of a bookseller and studied for a while at Oxford, until lack of money on the death of his father forced him to leave. He became a teacher and writer and moved to London in 1737. He wrote for *The Gentleman's Magazine* and helped to catalogue the library of the Earl of Oxford.

Johnson produced his *Plan of a Dictionary of the English Language* in 1747, a contract was signed and the first of his assistants began work that year. It took three years for him to read his source works and to mark the quotations to be used. These were copied out on to separate slips of paper by his assistants and filed in alphabetical order. Once this was completed, he began to draft his definitions. The work was completed by 1754 and an edition of 2000 copies was published in 1755. A much revised edition appeared in 1773. Johnson's dictionary was the first to portray the complexity of the lexicon of English and of English usage accurately and his use of quotations started a practice which has been used by dictionary compilers ever since. Most of Johnson's choices of spelling have remained and are to be found in modern practice. It is for this mammoth work that he is most generally remembered.

After the dictionary was completed he continued to write for literary journals as well as poetry, prose, biography and the famous travel journal, J*ourney to the Western Isles of Scotland*, which he undertook with Boswell as his companion. We know a good deal about Johnson as a person because of the work of Boswell, who became his biographer.

Johnson's later work included an eight-volume edition of Shakespeare's plays and a ten volume *Lives of the Most Eminent English Poets.*

He was given an honorary doctorate by Trinity College, Dublin (1765) and by Oxford in 1775. Thus he came to be Dr Johnson, the title by which he is most widely known. He died in 1784.

Spelling and vocabulary
Glossary

Accent – a matter of pronunciation; the way in which words are pronounced.

Affix – units of meaning which can be added both before and after the root of a word, for example, *un-/-ful.*

Alliteration – a sequence of words beginning with the same sound; occurs when adjacent words in a phrase start with the same phoneme.

Antonym – a word which has the opposite meaning to another word.

Ascender – many letters are the same height when written or printed on a line; some have a part, known as the ascender, which extends above this level: *b, d, f, h, i, k, l, t*. See also 'descender'.

Assonance – a device used in poetry, when the sound repeated is a phoneme within words, rather than at the end.

Blend – two or more separate phonemes blended together, especially at the beginnings and endings of words, for example, be**st** (*/s/* + */t/* blend), **str**ing (*/s/* + */t/* + */r/* blend). Also called consonant clusters.

Cliché – words or expressions which have lost much of their force through over-exposure; they are considered to be hackneyed and trite.

Colloquialism – a word or phrase which would be appropriate in conversation or in an informal situation, but is not appropriate in writing.

Compound word – the combination of two words to create a new word with a new meaning: *wind* + *mill* = *windmill*.

Consonant – sounds (phonemes) made when tongue, teeth or lips impede the air flow in speech. All the letters except *a, e, i, o, u* represent consonants. The letter y can be either consonant or vowel.

Cursive script – handwritten script in which the letters are joined.

Descender – the part of a written or printed letter which goes below the line level: *g, j, p, q, y*. See also 'ascender'.

Dialect – regional variations in vocabulary and grammar; usually spoken forms. Standard English is a dialect which is not regional.

Digraph – two letters (graphs) representing a single phoneme, for example, *ch-*, representing */ch/*, as in **church**.

Diphthong – a particular kind of vowel digraph. When a diphthong is articulated the shape of the mouth changes as the sound is made and it is possible to distinguish the two sounds gliding together, for example, *boil, road, pain*.

Etymology – the study of the history and origin of words.

Figurative language – the use of simile, metaphor, personification to create an impression or mood.

Genre – a text type; a particular kind of writing with distinctive characteristics of structure, vocabulary or patterns of language.
Grapheme – the written representation of a sound (phoneme); may consist of one or more letters (NLS, 1998).

Half-rhyme – words having vowel phonemes or sounds which are similar, but not the same, for example, Wales/shells.
Headword – words which are given at the top of each page in a dictionary to show which word appears at the start of the page and which at the end.
Homograph – a word with the same spelling as another, but with a different meaning. Pronunciation may also be different.
Homonym – a word with the same spelling or pronunciation as another, but with a different meaning or origin. Can be a homograph or homophone.
Homophones – words which sound the same but have different meanings or different spellings.

Idiom – a combination of words with a special meaning that cannot be inferred from its parts; the meanings of the words are not interpreted literally.
Imagery – 'the use of language to create a vivid sensory image' (NLS, 1998); writing which conveys ideas or feelings through the image presented. The image is usually visual but can also appeal to the other senses.

Metaphor – when a 'writer writes about something as if it were really something else' (NLS, 1998).
Mnemonic – comes from a Greek word which means 'remember'. In English, it means 'designed to aid the memory'.
Monosyllabic – words which have only one syllable.
Morpheme – the smallest unit of meaning in a word 'the smallest meaningful elements into which words can be analysed' (Crystal, 1987).
Morphology – the study of the structure of words.

Neologism – a newly coined word or a familiar word or phrase used in a new sense.

Onomatopoeia – where words are used to recreate particular sounds associated with their meanings, for example, *hiss, boom.*
Onset/rime – onset is the consonant or cluster of consonants at the beginning of a word or syllable and rime is the rest of this word or syllable, which enables it to rhyme with other words.
Orthography – the study of spelling; the principles underlying spelling.

Palindrome – a word or a phrase which is the same when read or spelled from left to right or right to left.

Personification – the attribution of human characteristics to 'non-human agents or objects or abstract concepts' (NLS, 1998).

Phoneme – the smallest unit of sound which changes the meaning of a word.

Phonology – the study of the sound systems of the language as they relate to meaning.

Phonics – 'the relationship between print symbol and sound patterns' (DfEE, 1995).

Plural – a form of a verb or noun which shows that more than one person or thing is involved.

Polysyllabic – words having more than one syllable.

Portmanteau – an alternative term for a lexical blend – a combination of two words to express a new concept, for example, *motel, brunch*.

Prefix – a unit of meaning (affix) which is added before the root of a word, to create a word with a new meaning, for example, *un-, dis-, de-*.

Proverb – a short, pithy phrase or sentence which expresses some kind of commonly held belief or traditional wisdom.

Rhyme – words which have the same sound in the final syllable.

Root word/base word – the root/base to which affixes can be added to create new words.

Simile – when 'the writer creates an image in readers' minds by comparing a subject to something else' (NLS, 1998).

Singular – a form of a verb or noun which shows there is only one person or thing involved.

Slang – language of a highly colloquial type, considered to be below the level of educated standard speech, and consisting either of new words or of current words employed in some special sense.

Standard English (SE) – is the usual dialect of written English and its linguistic features are matters of grammar, vocabulary and orthography. SE is not a matter of pronunciation. SE can be spoken with any accent.

Suffix – unit of meaning (affix) which is added after the root of a word, to create a word with a new meaning, for example, *-ful, -ing, -er*.

Syllable – a rhythmic segment of a word. A syllable must contain a vowel phoneme. A single syllable can have a number of consonants but it can have only one vowel phoneme.

Synonyms – words which have the same meaning; in most cases there are slight nuances of meaning or of emphasis which are different.

Thesaurus – a specific kind of dictionary containing lists of synonyms and related words.

Trigraph – three letters (graphs) representing a single phoneme, for example, *-igh* representing */ie/*, as in *high*.

Vowel – a speech sound which is produced without obstruction from tongue, teeth, lips. Vowel phonemes are represented in writing by single vowel letters *(a, e, i, o, u)* or combinations of vowels or vowels and consonants.

Spelling and vocabulary
INDEX